# Behind Closed Doors

## Find Healing from Domestic Abuse

## Alison Reid

## Onwards and Upwards Publishers

3 Radfords Turf, Cranbrook, Exeter,
EX5 7DX, United Kingdom.
www.onwardsandupwards.org

First edition. Published in the United Kingdom by Onwards and Upwards Publishers Ltd. (2019).

ISBN:              978-1-78815-727-8
Typeface:          Sabon LT
Graphic design:    LM Graphic Design

*The views and opinions expressed in this book are the author's own, and do not necessarily represent the views and opinions of Onwards and Upwards Publishers or its staff.*

*Although the author and publisher have made every effort to ensure that the information in this book was correct at press time, the author and publisher do not assume and hereby disclaim any liability to any party for any loss, damage, or disruption caused by errors or omissions, whether such errors or omissions result from negligence, accident, or any other cause.*

*This book is not intended as a substitute for the advice of a counsellor. The reader should regularly consult a professional in matters relating to his/her emotional health and particularly with respect to any symptoms that may require diagnosis or special attention.*

Unless otherwise specified, scripture quotations are taken from the Holy Bible, New International Version® Anglicized, NIV® Copyright © 1979, 1984 by Biblica, Inc.® Used by permission. All rights reserved worldwide. Scripture quotations marked (AMP) are taken from the Amplified® Bible, Copyright © 1987 by The Lockman Foundation. Used by permission. www.Lockman.org. Scripture quotations marked (KJV) are from The Authorized (King James) Version. Rights in the Authorized Version in the United Kingdom are vested in the Crown. Reproduced by permission of the Crown's patentee, Cambridge University Press. Scripture quotations marked (MSG) are taken from THE MESSAGE. Copyright © by Eugene H. Peterson 1993, 1994, 1995, 1996, 2000, 2001, 2002. Used by permission of NavPress. All rights reserved. Represented by Tyndale House Publishers, Inc. Scripture quotations marked (TNIV) are taken from Today's New International® Version TNIV©. Copyright 2001, 2005 by International Bible Society®. All rights reserved worldwide.

# Endorsements

An authentic testimony of brokenness to beauty. This book shares personal experience from survival of abuse and clearly demonstrates to the reader a Biblical perspective promoting healing and restoration. This sensitively written narrative gives inspiration and hope for those experiencing abuse.

### T. Knight, BA Counselling MBACP (Accredited)

This book isn't always an easy read; it has come through great trials, but by grace has become a story of victory and freedom. It came through great personal pain to Alison, but by grace she has turned that cost into a gift – a moving testimony of God's love and healing. Alison writes this from a call to "bring liberty to the captives" and writes with authenticity and authority.

Though it deserves a wider audience, this book is especially a gift to anyone who might be currently experiencing, or has experienced, domestic abuse, or who knows someone who has. It offers divine inspiration and earthly wisdom. In Alison's own words, "This healing … is real; I am a witness to that." Praise God.

### Rev. M. Tufnell

Finding Healing from Domestic Abuse

# Acknowledgements

A huge thank you to all my faithful friends, who through their continued love, support, encouragement and especially prayers made this book (and my life) possible.

A very grateful thank you to my dear friend T. Knight for writing the review but most importantly for being such a lovely, kind, faithful and gentle friend to me.

Thank you so much to a true 'good shepherd', the Rev. Mike Tufnell, for his time and his kind and encouraging endorsement. His servant-hearted kindness, wisdom, sincerity and discernment are a shining example to our very blessed church.

Thank you to Luke, editor extraordinaire, for your vision, faith, patience and excellent skills.

Thank you to David, my husband, the handsome rock. For your strong faith in a loving God. For all your love, kindness, support and encouragement in our life journey together and for your unfaltering belief in me. The respect you show all women should be an inspiration to all men.

Lastly, thank you to the lover of my soul, Father, Son and Spirit, to the One without whom nothing is possible and with whom 'all things are possible'. Your love is King.

*To my Grandma, Violet,
for your consistent love and
understanding throughout my
childhood and for being a beacon
of strength, warmth and joy.*

*Until we meet again in heaven.*

*Love you, Grandma.*

# Contents

Preface ...............................................................................9

Introduction ...................................................................11

PART ONE: MY STORY ....................................................17

1. The Handsome Stranger ............................................19

2. A Storm Warning – Recognising the Signs .................28

3. Bad Hair Day ...........................................................48

4. Sweet Talker ............................................................53

5. Mind Games ............................................................61

6. Paranoia..................................................................65

7. My Testimony...........................................................72

PART TWO: MANUAL OF HOPE ........................................79

8. Freedom..................................................................81

9. Tender to my Daughters............................................88

10. The Bible as a Weapon............................................98

11. An Encouraging Bible Study ...................................106

12. Healing.................................................................122

13. Jesus Believed in Emotional Healing .......................134

14. A Note to the Perpetrators......................................143

Helpful Resources.........................................................148

Afterword.....................................................................151

Contact the Author.......................................................152

Finding Healing from Domestic Abuse

# Preface

## In the beginning

> *And the Lord turned to me and said;*
> *Write the vision and engrave it so plainly upon tablets that*
> *everyone who passes may read as they hasten by.*
>
> *Habakkuk 2:2-3 (AMP)*

It is a grey November day and I'm sitting in my friend Chrissie's cosy living room.

'Well, Ali, what are you going to *do* with your life?'

I'm silent. I have *no* idea.

I'm in my forties and jobless. My career as a Registered Nurse is over as I've injured my back. I've lost both my parents, and my husband and I are childless, so there's no one to look after. I've just finished a degree in Theology, which I had hoped would spark some ideas of what to do next in life, but nothing has inspired me. I have no plans or ideas for the future.

We decide to pray for some inspiration (always a good idea).

'Do you do any writing?' Chrissie asks. My heart starts to thump with excitement and anticipation. As a child and young adult, I used to love to write. Books and reading are a love I share with my mum but since she has died many years before, my writing seems to have died with her. Chrissie continues in prayer:

'I have a picture of you writing a book or a programme for women who have been caught in domestic abuse.'

It seems impossible to me at the time.

## Why, Lord?

It's true that I have suffered from a childhood of awful domestic abuse at my father's hands, but I don't know why God would pick me to write about this. Surely, there are so many other women with similar experiences who would be better writers, or more knowledgeable or wise or spiritual?

But, there is one thing I do know.

I know that since I suffered those days of unholy pain and fear, the Lord has unswervingly and faithfully continued to heal and restore me, piece by piece. He's always done it in His own way and in His own time. Sometimes much to my frustration or tears, but He has done it perfectly. He has shown Himself faithful.

The other thing I know is that if you have had similar hurts or traumas, His desire is to restore you completely too.

The Lord is appalled at the abuse you may have suffered (whether slight or huge) and He doesn't condone or agree with it. Within His horror at your abuse is also His mercy and love that absolutely desires to see you healed and made whole again. So that you might live as Jesus said: 'life to its fullest'[1]. He has 'good plans for you, plans to prosper you and not to harm you'[2] and He wants you to have an abundantly good, happy and satisfying life in 'good measure, shaken down and running over'[3].

---

[1] Jn. 10:10
[2] Jer. 29:11
[3] Lk. 6:38

# Introduction

*There is no fear in love. But perfect love drives out fear, because fear has to do with punishment. The one who fears is not made perfect in love.*

*1 John 4:18*

## Whom this book is for

I have written this book primarily for women who are suffering from domestic abuse or, like me, have done so in the past. (I am aware that males suffer abuse too, which is equally horrendous, but I feel that my calling is to females. Therefore, I use the language of 'male perpetrator against female' throughout the book.)

I am the first to admit that I am not a qualified expert on domestic abuse nor do I have any professional knowledge of this area, but I have suffered from it. I believe that God will speak to you through this book, and my prayer is that He will inspire you as you read and pray and make yourself open to all that He has to say to you. The Lord will work differently with everyone because He respects our individuality, but His goal is that you step into complete freedom and peace. However, it will be 'not by might, nor by power but by my Spirit'[4].

Through reading this book, hopefully you will also realise that you are not alone: that others have had the same abuse; that others have managed to escape; and ultimately, that others have been healed, made whole and set free to live and love again. Last but not least, you will know (and I can't stress this strongly enough) that *there is hope.*

*So, keep going, keep strong and break free into all the good things that God has for you.*

## Disclaimer

*We were by nature, objects of wrath.*

*Ephesians 2:3*

---

[4] Zechariah 4:6

This book is mainly personal testimony of how I viewed my father and his behaviours. I have intentionally aimed to write this book as honestly as possible. (Occasionally, however, I may have left extra details out or changed names if it seemed necessary.)

Therefore, I have purposefully kept in some of the 'ugly truths' about my thoughts and language, or that of my parents. I haven't done this to intentionally offend anyone but merely because I wanted this account to be real and how I remember it. However, I am sorry if any of our attitudes, behaviour or language upsets you.

## A lifetime away

I have been blessed with nearly thirty years of fairly regular and persistent psychological and spiritual healing and 'normal' secular counselling. So much so that when it came to realising that the Lord was wanting me to write my story, I honestly thought there was no way that I could do it.

You see, the Lord had done so much healing work in me that although I had not forgotten the things in this book, so many of them seemed a lifetime – or even someone else's lifetime – away. The pain and the suffering had gone, and I felt at peace. The effects of most of the tortures of abuse (and it *is* torture) have been healed, and the woman who writes these words now bears little resemblance to the girl that many of these stories are about. Later in the book I will talk about these healings.

However, some of them are so deep it is impossible to put them into words. Yet I *know* that they've taken place. I *know* that I am more whole and happy, secure and at peace than I have ever been, from deep within my heart and soul to even my outward appearance.

## The rose called 'forgiveness'

Both of my parents passed away some years ago, but I can honestly say that I have no malice or anger toward them now. I really can bless them for all that was good in them, and there was much. My parents weren't monsters; they were as all of us: fallen human beings, open to both evil and good, as we choose.

I am convinced that forgiveness is essential to life. I have forgiven both my parents (and have had to keep on forgiving them) until that forgiveness has taken root: a beautiful rose that blossoms purely because of Jesus' sacrifice and grace, and not through my own striving.

## Interested parties

I have also written this book for those of you who have not suffered domestic abuse (and hopefully never will) but have an interest in the subject. I am hoping that it will help you to understand how abusive men 'work' at the abuse and it will give you a little taster as to how it feels to be in a relationship with one.

If you are reading this because you can see a loved one heading toward the rocks of this type of relationship, do send up some danger flares and warn her. However, if she doesn't heed your warnings, then do still please be there for her – a close lifeboat coming alongside, once she's ready to climb in.

This message comes with a warning though. Please don't try to grab out and rescue her to pull her in, or she (or her abuser) might well drown you too. Unfortunately, you can't save her. *She has to do that for herself.* But you can be a lifeline for her, to be on her side when she needs you, either practically or emotionally.[5]

## The factual bit

> *For wisdom will enter your heart, and knowledge will be pleasant to your soul. Discretion will protect you, and understanding will guard your heart.*
>
> *Proverbs 2:10,11*

I am aware that there are many men that suffer domestic abuse at the hands of their wives or partners. Obviously, I have enormous sympathy for their situations too and if this book can help any of them, then that would be especially wonderful.

However, statistically, the figures for male against female abuse are dramatically higher than the other way around. For example, worldwide, women (between the ages of 15-44) are more likely to be maimed or

---

[5] Susan Brewster's book *To be an Anchor in the Storm* is a good reference guide, if you want practical help for this.

killed by their 'loving' partners than by the combination of war, traffic accidents, cancer and malaria.[6]

In the UK the statistics are equally as horrifying. Two women are murdered by their partners every week.[7] Every six seconds a woman is assaulted in her home.[8] One in four women will suffer domestic abuse at some point in their lifetime.[9] Also, bear in mind that these are just the statistics that we know about; surveys indicate that 50% of women will never tell anyone about the abuse that they have suffered.[10]

This book does not contain qualified professional guidance about your abuser or how to leave him. There are some amazing organisations and books that deal with this advice far more effectively and knowledgably than I can.[11]

This book will help you to recognise the signs of an abuser, explaining how they work and the effects on those they abuse. It also aims to show how God can heal those painful effects of abuse and give new freedom and joy to anyone who's been unfortunate enough to have gone through it.

*It is a manual of hope.*

## A note of caution

A note of caution is needed for those who read this and determine to leave their abuser, and for those who have loved ones whom they want to help leave an abusive relationship.

My intention is not to frighten anyone, but I do believe that we are called to be mature and wise. Statistically, 75% of the murders that occur in abusive relationships, between male abuser and female victim, happen when the woman tries to leave (or has left) the relationship.[12]

---

[6] UN 2007, taken from the 'Statistics' section on page 5 of the *Ending Domestic Abuse: A Pack for Churches* PDF produced by Restored.

[7] Women's Aid 2010, from page 5 of the *Ending Domestic Abuse: A Pack for Churches* PDF produced by Restored

[8] Professor Stanko, E.; *The Day to Count: A Snapshot of the Impact of Domestic Violence in the UK;* Criminal Justice, 1:2 (2000); taken from Craven, Pat; *Living with the Dominator;* page 111.

[9] Home Office (2007)

[10] Anderson, Jocelyn; *Woman Submit!;* page 77.

[11] See further reading list on page 145.

[12] *www.domesticabuseshelter.org/InfoDomesticViolence.htm#statistics,* accessed July 2014

If you decide to escape your abuser, then that is wonderful news. But *please, please, please* be wise about it. You are the best authority on how to keep yourself safe. Ideally, seek professional advice on how to do this. But if that is not possible, I would advise you to take your time *(unless of course your life or that of your children is in immediate danger)* and *plan your escape.* Do lots of research and contact organisations or charities[13] on how to do this safely. Try to find trustworthy friends or family to confide in who may be able to offer you a lifeline if needed.

If you are an interested party and desperate to help an abused loved one, then equally please *be very wise.* What you might see as kind and helpful words and actions might be the very thing that causes your loved one more hurt or may even threaten her or your own life.

This is not to dissuade you from helping her or to make you despair at her situation. Quite the opposite; as I have mentioned before, you can be a lifeline to that person. But it will require you to act in a way that will ease her situation, to not dominate her or put her unwittingly into danger. Bear in mind, also, that she may well test your patience by continually returning to her abuser. Statistically, an abused woman will return to her abuser up to fifteen times before she will permanently leave him. But, please don't give up on her; you may well save her and her children's lives.

## Prayer

*Heavenly Father,*

*Thank you that you know me, you love me and accept me just the way I am. Please would you speak to me through this book and help me to hear all that you want to say to me. Lord Jesus, thank you that you want me to have a good, happy and abundant life. Please help me to start to step into all of the good things that you have for me and allow you to heal and restore me in body, mind and spirit. Thank you, Lord.*

*Amen.*

---

[13] See the list on page 147, for example.

Finding Healing from Domestic Abuse

# PART ONE

# My Story

# CHAPTER ONE

# The Handsome Stranger

*Wisdom will save you from the ways of wicked men, from men whose words are perverse, who leave the straight paths to walk in dark ways, who delight in doing wrong.*

*Proverbs 2:12*

The tall, suave, good-looking man jauntily crosses the quiet main road in the small country market town. He looks into the estate agents' window at his friend sitting behind the desk and he waves to him. It's the end of a hard-working day and they share a joke and confirm their usual drinking appointment in the local men's club the following Thursday, all by joyful hand signals through the window.

Next, he approaches the newsagents, just as a young mother pushing a pram gets to the door and, sweeping her a devastating smile, he holds the door open for her with a gallant relish, whilst winking at her bedazzled toddler. The mum smiles shyly, instantly drawn to this handsome, jolly, polite stranger, and goes about her day with an extra spring in her step. The newsagent knows this man and chats fondly with him about his family and a joyous interchange takes place.

'What a pleasant man!' is what the world – his friends, the young mother and the newsagent – around him think. No, they don't just *think* it; they *know* it! They know it because they've seen the evidence; he is a smiling, happy, polite, kind man with a wonderful family and friends. What's not to like? 'If only more people could be like him, the world would be such a better place,' they reason to themselves. 'Not only does he act handsomely but he looks the part too.'

The handsome man now makes his way home. 'Home' is a large and extremely modern house that he designed and built himself with his own hands. His neighbours and friends look at it and wonder at this guy's talents; not only is he an arty, sensitive guy, but he's practical too. Is there no end to his talents and accomplishments? He's athletic-looking and sporty, with a pretty, intelligent, buxom blonde wife and three handsome, obedient and bright children. He's a bit like James Bond: men want to be him, women want to sleep with him and children wish he could be their exciting dad. The man enters the kitchen of his beautiful home and sees his children and wife waiting for him.

*His manner instantly becomes aloof.* Gone are the smiles and charm. His face is like concrete, hard and impenetrable, and his eyes hold a vicious light. His body language speaks of being incredibly tense as though every bone, sinew and muscle of his six-foot-two Navy-fit frame is taut and pent up. He appears to seethe with unleashed anger.

He slowly and menacingly draws his chair out from under the kitchen table. His teeth are gritted and his body holds disgust at being with these people i.e. his family. He doesn't acknowledge or even look at his wife and it's as if his children do not exist. The children, who were loud, energetic and having fun before he arrived, have become completely withdrawn and silent. They do not dare to speak to him or look directly at him.

His pretty blonde wife, who has been caring for their three children and working as a secretary all day, has spent the last drops of the evening and her energy cooking his meal. Despite him ignoring her, she tries to appease him with gentle language and tones whilst she finishes preparing the dinner.

His family are not allowed to start eating until he is home – no matter how late. She places his dinner down in front of him first, because he *must* be served first. He looks at his plate and his face becomes instantly contorted with infinite horror and reproach. He thinks, 'How dare she serve me cheap supermarket pizza!' He springs aggressively to his feet, the upturned chair crashing to the floor behind him. The children jump. He accusingly points to his plate, roaring his head off, shouting and swearing.

'I'm not eating this b****y s**t!'

His wife sits at the table rigid with fear and dread, powerless to speak or act. The children instantly scan for their exit routes. Their eyes are wide with survival. Their bodies pulsate with horror and adrenaline as they aim to keep themselves alive for another day.

He grabs the plate of pizza and sends it hurling towards the far wall. It whistles just over the children's heads and sends the poor startled cat springing off the piano for cover. His family gaze at him in horror...

Welcome home, Dad!

## My dad

*He is a double minded man, unstable in all he does.*

James 1:8

I opened this book by writing 'The Handsome Stranger' story as I wanted you as the reader to enter this world with a tiny taster of the chaotic feelings that surround those who are involved in a relationship with this type of man. How can this man who is so charming and attractive to the outside world be the same man who treats his family in such a despicable way?

'The Handsome Stranger' story is actually factual. My poor hard-working mum had served shop-made pizza (instead of homemade) one evening and my dad reacted by swearing and throwing it at the wall. This was what life was like for us all. To the outside world this man, my dad, was above reproach. He *really was* kind, fun, popular and charming. However, to us who were his 'loved ones', he also *really was* a sadistic monster that shared our home. To live with this man *was* shocking.

## Dad's history

My father was sporty, lively, attractive, outgoing and fun. His lifestyle was that of a successful businessman, with parties and social events, clubs and dinners. We weren't rich but compared to where his parents had come from, we weren't poor. (My grandma had come from mixed Irish and Cornish descendants who had ended up in a poverty-stricken area of Bethnal Green in London's East End, and my grandpa came from Aberdeen, in Scotland.)

However, my grandparents had worked hard, and my grandpa had ended up working in the Bank of England, in London (in his natty lemon-coloured spats!) Growing up, my dad had wanted for nothing. As a young man he had been good at sport and studying and so had gone to grammar school. He grew into manhood during the Second World War and went into the Royal Navy where he became a real 'macho man'. (He never wore deodorant or jewellery as he said it was for sissies!)

But Dad had also been good at art and design, so after the War he went on to study to become an architect. He was healthy and fit and had a beautiful, loving wife and three children. He was blessed. Yet, the reality was that despite all of the good things that life had given him, he was sadistic, especially to those whom he 'cared' about or 'loved' most.

This is the frustrating truth about this type of man. So many of them have everything going for them and yet they can't seem to help acting out of this ugly, evil side of their nature. *Or can they?*

In my opinion, these abusers are devastatingly good actors and deadly manipulators whose whole life, if not their character, is often built upon a lie. Unless you are absolutely on guard, they will suck you in.

Whilst some think that they are not able to help their behaviours, the majority of research shows that they know *exactly* what they are doing. Everything in their lives and characters, from the way they use their body language to the very specific words they use, is calculated, and this calculation starts from the first day of meeting you, irrespective of who you are.[14]

## Types of abusive men

*A fool gives full vent to his anger, but a wise man keeps himself under control.*

*Proverbs 29:11*

I have purposely written about my dad being a specific 'type' of man. I believe (as do experts that work in this field) that men that indulge in domestic abuse are of a particular 'type'. Therefore, although they may use differing techniques to get what they want, their underlying behaviours and characters are very similar.[15]

All of these men use a campaign of domination, manipulation and control in order to achieve their goals. These tactics usually include a mixture of several types of abuse toward you, your children or loved ones.

- *Psychological attacks:* verbal abuse, slander, derogatory comments about your appearance or abilities (weight and cooking are favourites); denial; sulking; 'gas-lighting' (a term coined from

---

[14] See further reading list: Don Hennessy's book, *How He Gets Into Her Head,* is excellent for more information on perpetrators.

[15] Craven, Pat; *Living with the Dominator;* Freedom Publishing (UK, 2008).

a film about a husband who tried to send his wife mad by denying reality); being kind/loving one minute and cruel the next; silence, ignoring etc.

- *Threatening or controlling behaviours:* shouting, swearing, glaring; threatening to take your children away; treating you as a slave; isolating you from friends and family; stopping you working; controlling your money, phone, clothes, choices; threatening suicide or to kill your children if you leave; demanding sex, denying sex etc.
- *Physical violence:* punching, kicking, slapping, strangling, hair-pulling; rape; pushing down stairs; breaking things (including things you particularly need, want or are attached to); attacking you when you are pregnant etc.

Nearly all of these behaviours will be done at home 'behind closed doors' with probably no outside witnesses, if he can help it.

## Empowering information

This idea that perpetrators of abuse are a 'type' *is powerful* (and the one thing that these men don't want you to have is power). No longer can his abuse be blamed on you! He no longer has any excuses; even if he insists that his abuse is purely down to him just being temperamental, insecure, jealous, passionate, artistic or even drunk.

This type of man has form; he's done it before, and there are many who are just like him and there always have been throughout history. Use the power of this information, then, to take the best possible course of action to ensure that he is unable to trick, brainwash or seduce you any further. You are now able to see through his mask. *You are not responsible for his behaviour.*

## Street angel, home devil

To the world outside your doors, these men often appear as perfectly decent and respectable people. They use the realms of deception, lies and charm in order to achieve this. They appear to be one thing but are really another, the iconic Jekyll and Hyde. They will do it incredibly subtly as they are masters at their game.

This is how they continue their patterns of abuse and seduction with *everyone* that they meet. Please don't think of seduction just in terms of sex; many of the men that they meet as friends or work colleagues will be just as seduced into thinking of him as a really sound, dependable guy.

Although there are so many more good, stable, kind, supportive and loving men in the world than there are abusers, please be aware that they are around. They could be your new partner or a neighbour, a friend, a pastor, a colleague or family member. Determine that you'll not be seduced by him and that you'll watch out for those that are.

## Can't help loving that man of mine

As you can imagine, to fall in love with this type of man and to end up marrying him or living with him is dangerous and costly. He is completely double-sided. To live with him is to be constantly wrong-footed initially; until you can learn to read him, you will never know which side is the one you will get that day. One minute you are being seduced by this attractive, kind, charming and gracious man. The next you are absolutely flabbergasted and appalled as this beautiful man changes before your eyes. He becomes perverted and dangerous, a threatening, frightening animal of a man.

Is this too strong a description? If you are saying that, I can tell that you've never lived with an abuser or encountered one in full throttle (pardon the pun). If you have, you won't be shocked or offended but will just be sadly nodding your head in agreement. As a child or as an adult living with and loving this type of man, everything in the world constantly changes and makes even the littlest things seem unstable.

He purposely changes your perception of everything and takes away your ability to reason. It is a form of brainwashing. You question everything: *What is the truth? Did I say that? Did I do that? What is reliable? Whom can I trust?* And even, most disturbingly, *what is reality?*

It is his intention to keep you like this, unsure of what he will do or say next. You are aware that *anything* can make him volatile and at any time. Hence a lot of women describe living with this man as 'walking on eggshells'.

His intention is to make you feel unstable, unsure, at risk, not just in your physical safety but also in your psychological safety. You are not able to trust that he will remain stable. You are not even able to trust that your own thoughts and logic will remain stable. He literally 'messes with your mind'. Your world is in constant chaos, a ragged ship raging through storms with nothing tied down and no one seemingly steering at the helm.

Once he has you trapped in his 'loving' web of lies he will insist that he is perfectly normal and that *you* are the one who is at fault.

## You are not!

I cannot say this strongly enough but,

> You are not, never have been and never will be responsible for *any* of his behaviours.
>
> He is an adult and completely responsible for *all* of his behaviours.

I go into more detail about this at the end of the book, but if you have been abused by him just let these true facts start to enter your mind to come against all the brainwashing you have had to withstand.

## Out of the mouths of babes

*They are the kind who worm their way into homes.*

*2 Timothy 3:6*

As the child of an abuser rather than a lover, I obviously don't know what it's like to have met one as an adult or to have been seduced into a 'loving relationship' with one. As such, I can't write from that perspective.

Due to a childhood of abuse, as I became a teenager I taught myself how to avoid this sort of abusive man when I met new people. I knew instinctively that if ever I was strongly physically attracted to a man or he had a type of magnetic pull over me, that he was probably bad news! The few lads I did chose to go out with (or rather, who chose me, as I was too shy and insecure to go after any) were always sweet and kind. The minute any man showed signs of dominance or unkindness, one of us would be out of the door.

However, I do believe that being a child of an abuser rather than a lover has in some ways given me the chance to be objective about these men. I haven't had the complications of falling in love with a man who at first was amazing and gentle, only to turn into a sadist once he had trapped me. I haven't had to suffer being raped by my husband or all the other hideous things that go with being 'in love' with an abuser.

As a child I still suffered the psychological and physical abuse but I also had the ability to observe my dad without the complications of loving him as a lover. Unwittingly, I studied his behaviours and patterns over the approximately twenty years I lived with him. (Most children of abusers do this as it's the only way to survive the danger.)

As I studied him there were certain facts that I picked up about his behaviour. Firstly, I realised the fact that however out of control, violent, random or 'in a temper' he appeared, the truth was that he was actually (chillingly) always *in control of himself* and secondly, *all of his behaviour was intentional.*

I observed that his violent outbursts and anger were just as much part of his dominating plan as were his quieter patterns of continuous put-downs and verbal abuse. They were all geared to undermine our power and self-worth and to feed his. If his behaviour had been spontaneous and out of his control then what could account for these following facts:

- He never showed that side of himself (his violence and aggressive put-downs) to anyone outside the four closest members of the family. None of our extended family or even his closest friends (as far as I know) had witnessed these violent outbursts, despite having been in circumstances that at home would normally have 'set him off'.
- His behaviour was such an act that I could copy it back to him, mimicking his physicality, his gestures, his language, even appearing in a temper when I wasn't. (This is exactly what I used to do; I put on the same act of moving aggressively, shouting, swearing, seething with anger, being intimidating *towards him*. This was my defence system, fighting fire with fire.)

## Give that man an Oscar!

I believe that the knowledge that I have gained from observing my dad's acting skills is useful to any of you that are being abused now or have suffered abuse. As previously mentioned, perpetrators of abuse will use brainwashing techniques to try to get you to believe that the abuse that they dish out is 'all your fault'. They insist that they have no control over themselves and that if only you were different (more beautiful, more loving, more kind, more gentle, more understanding, more faithful, a better cook), if only you weren't so fat, petty, flat-chested, didn't nag, hadn't switched the light off, flirted with that man, broken the window, cooked that dinner, bumped the car, 'looked at me that way', worn that skirt, and so on, then they wouldn't have lost control. Every single 'reason' is a lie but it helps to keep you in his prison of domination.

Let this truth start to sink into your mind as I continue with my story and some of the things that happened in my childhood. If you have or are being abused at present, see if any of them 'ring any bells' for you? If they do, then good; as I have said, you are starting to recognise your abuser's 'type' and you will loosen the grip that he has on you.

Don't be frightened to try to gain your freedom back. Keep strong; you deserve a good life.

# CHAPTER TWO

# A Storm Warning – Recognising the Signs

*Do not envy a violent man. Or choose any of his ways.*

*Proverbs 3:31*

The next six chapters contain short true stories or facts about what it was like to live in a 'home' with a Jekyll and Hyde type father. I put 'home' into quotation marks because in no way does living with a perpetrator feel like a safe, warm, cosy and relaxing home. It can be more like a house of horrors.

I've written these stories as signposts. These will hopefully point you in the direction of recognising similar behaviours and styles in your own abuser, whether physical or psychological. This will help you to identify them as a perpetrator and that you are, or have been, in an abusive relationship (or if you've not suffered abuse, to show you what it is like to live with one).

Many of the stories are about my childhood or adolescence, and if children have been involved in any of that abuse (whether that be directly or as observers), bear in mind that they might be undergoing similar traumas to my own.

The sections will run chronologically through my life from childhood to adulthood.

## Living in Jekyll and Hyde's house

Living with Dad as a child growing up was like being on the merry-go-round from hell. When you are little, this merry- (or misery-) go-round is dark and evil. It has frightening, fire-breathing, rabid horses painted in blacks and reds. It is a constant cycle of emotional ups and downs, and a never-ending round and round, yet with the same patterns.

It never stops and it never gives you a chance to get off. You are caught and have no choices.

His moods follow a pattern. There will be times when he will be the life and soul of the party: chatting, friendly, outgoing, jolly, kind, even generous occasionally. These lull and tempt you into a false sense of security. They make you want to put all your guards down.

You're partly tempted to relax because these times are so nice you want to believe that they will go on forever and that he has changed. They are lulling, because after the exhaustion of battle they are a welcome rest and unless you become steel-like in your determination not to trust him again, they can easily persuade you that he's become a decent human being.

After one of these good periods, though, the mood starts to change and he starts to darken. It is the menacing calm before the storm. Gone is my friendly and kind dad; now a man who bears no resemblance to him starts to darken our door.

He starts by withdrawing, hardly speaking and becoming gruff and moody when he does speak. Nothing and no one can satisfy him or bring him out of this and everything starts to become a problem. The mood in the house becomes ominous. It is dark and electric with the promise of impending horror. This may go on for weeks or days depending entirely on a logic known only to him. He has no desire to come out of this place and no enticements of comfort, caring, understanding, having fun, distraction or threat will move him. He is resolute that he will stay there until he is ready.

When *he* is ready, the next phase will begin. If it were possible, the atmosphere in the house becomes even *more* threatening. Those dark clouds gathering have become deepest black and you know that an almighty storm is about to strike. His body language increases in tension and speaks of being pent up. Seething is held rigid in him, a coiled viper ready to spring.

Every physical motion that he does is done with thinly veiled anger and threat. He moves slower and more deliberately, a panther that is stalking his prey. Foreboding in his every intent, his facial expression is one of tight discontentment and complete disgust at whatever or whoever he looks at. (It's as though we, or something else, have done him an incredible injustice and caused him some excruciating pain that he can't hold back. He feels that rage is the only right expression of it, you can tell from his eyes.)

29

This stage of the misery-go-round may last minutes or days but not usually weeks (it would probably be too tiring for him, as this Oscar amount of acting can take some energy!) However, when he decides this time period will be over, he will start the next shift.

'It' will probably start with something banal. My brother Jon was once sworn and shouted at and then physically chased down the road by Dad for not 'eating his peas properly'. (Jon was mashing them down with his fork, that's all.) Jon got away and ran for three miles to the nearest town and the safety of his friend's house. We later learnt that he had not had time to put his shoes on and had run all the way there in bare feet. It was heartbreaking.

Dad's explosion can be created from anything he chooses to be wrong, whether that be a look from someone, an inanimate object in the wrong place, how a door is shut, time not being kept, 'incorrect' food. The list is endless and pitiful.

There is absolutely no rhyme or logic to this decision; therefore there is no point trying to waste energy in reasoning or using logic to 'help' him. Logic and reason don't work because he's chosen something illogical on purpose. (It's easier to throw you off track and make you doubt your own self and logic if it's completely unintelligible.) The chosen 'reason' will be explained, as his explosive reign of terror now begins.

## My house, my rules

> Listen, daughter, and pay careful attention;
> Forget your people and your father's house.
>
> *Psalm 45: 10-11*

There are *lots* of rules in our house. These rules have to be obeyed or they can actually hold not just serious and painful consequences but quite literally the death penalty. This seems a little extreme and yet, this is the reality for us who live there.

Sometimes, of course, these rules change according to the one who makes them, which makes them slippery shifting-sand rules. If any are broken, all hell can literally break loose. I have been smacked so hard round the face that the force of the blow has caused me to land six feet away from where I was standing because I've left my school bag by the front door or a mug in the sitting room.

Here are some of the rules that we have to abide by:

## The head of the table

My father has *his* chairs – one in the kitchen and one in the lounge. If you are sitting in one of *his* chairs and he enters the room, you learn to quickly vacate it. His chair is, of course, the biggest, most comfy and in the best position to see the TV. He decides what is watched on TV and the rest of us have to like it or lump it. 'My way or the highway' is one of his favourite phrases.

## My way or the highway to Hereford

Time must be strictly adhered too. So much so that he puts all the clocks in the house five minutes faster. Of course, we all know that they're five minutes fast so we just mentally take that time off, but on *no account* dare you be late! (My brother's wedding was in Hereford, four hours away by car. Dad insisted that the rest of the family had to leave our house at 5am to make sure we got there in time, despite me pointing out the logic that the wedding wasn't even until two and so we'd be hanging around for five hours. Sure enough, we arrived at 9am. My poor brother wasn't dressed, had just had breakfast and was on his way to the loo! He seemed a little surprised to see us.)

## The doors

Doors are very important in our house. Rule number one: they must remain shut in order to keep *his* privacy and the heating costs down. However, if one of *us* is on the phone in the hall (this is the good old days of static phones attached to lines) then mysteriously these same doors 'magically' open and remain open. They are opened – by him – so that in his paranoia he can keep tabs on what any of us are saying. He's a spy; but not a very good one, as I'm onto him.

Whenever one of us goes to answer the phone (he won't because he's got slaves – sorry, I mean *children* – to do it for him) we always shut the door behind us (in case we get shouted at later for leaving it open for the heat to escape; remember rule number one!) However, if the phone call is for one of us, he always seems to mysteriously need something from another room (though he always comes back empty-handed) and, guess what? After he returns to his room, he *doesn't* shut the door after himself! Horror! He's broken rule number one! He's broken it so that he can listen in to our calls. Different types of voyeurism are big news in our house.

I show the spy that I'm onto him; if the call is for me I explain to my friend and put the phone down on its side and purposely go and shut any door that has miraculously opened (as soon as it is safe and he's sat down after opening it!) He can't then come and open the door as that would be too obvious and of course go against rule number one. I do it to annoy him and to show him that I am onto him, as though that is going to somehow make him see the pointlessness of his paranoia. It doesn't; it just winds him up more, but I feel justified.

The energy that all of these games consume is phenomenal and they would be quite humorous if the results weren't life-threatening. I don't quite know what sort of paranoid thoughts he was having about our calls. I really am not plotting his downfall; I'm only arranging to meet a friend for a coffee.

## It's your fault

*No one should accuse or blame another person.*

*Hosea 4:4*

The blame game is also very popular. I have been blamed for pipes two feet from the toilet leaking because:

'You put the b****y toilet lid *down too hard!'*

Also for electrics failing, cars breaking, fairy lights going out, clocks telling the wrong time, cat's pooing, the house being too cold or too hot, not eating properly, stirring jam; the list is endless. All this 'power' to do wrong could go to a girl's head if it weren't nearly ripped off each time I'm at 'fault'.

## It must be you

Whenever Dad goes into blaming mode, his body and voice have one of two settings. He either does the low-menacing-voiced, tight-lipped, pent-up-anger style or he does the all-out, full-blown, swearing, shouting, violent style.

Either way, the magic finger is always involved. Have you ever seen the old World War I recruitment poster of the moustached man pointing a large finger at you the onlooker? My dad has that finger. That finger points at me frequently when I'm being accused of something – anything, in fact.

It tells me that he is boss, that he knows that I've 'done wrong' and that I'm about to be blamed for it (regardless of the truth). It tells me that I'm a lower human being and that I'm about to probably be beaten up for the imaginary wrong.

All the time he points, he is regardless of the old adage that for every finger you point to blame someone, there are three – of your own – fingers pointing back at you, the accuser. (Well, in his case five fingers pointing back at him, because out of sight I've probably flicked two of my own up at him in the process.)

## The age of innocence

*...you covered me in my mother's womb.*

*Psalm 139:13*

How my father hasn't killed me or my siblings, I'll never know. My siblings speak of kickings and beatings that made them literally see stars ('like Tom and Jerry,' my sister says). I've witnessed my brother Jon being kicked all the way up our hall – and it was a long hall – and miraculously his spleen has stayed intact.

My brother remembers him kicking my mum on the floor when she was pregnant with me. Jon tried to stop him but was thrown off. Apparently, this is a common act amongst this type of men. (A Refuge 2007 statistic states that abused women are three times more likely to be injured whilst pregnant.[16]) It has also been proven that this type of abuse has led to the child either aborting or being born with epilepsy or cerebral palsy.

As I look back over time, the fact that we weren't killed or too badly harmed physically is absolutely miraculous. *How can this be?* I don't recognise it yet but my lifesaver – my Saviour – has been at it again, rescuing me. One day I'll look back on all the times my dad could so easily have killed us and be thankful that He was there.

## The school run

*At that time I will deal with all who oppressed you.*

*Zephaniah 3:19*

---

[16] Taken from the 'Statistics' section on page 5 of the *Ending Domestic Abuse: A Pack for Churches* PDF produced by Restored.

The drive to school is a regular nightmare despite being brightened by the lovely Irish lilt of Terry Wogan on the radio! So much of a nightmare that when I'm older and at the comprehensive school, I will try as much as I can to walk to school; despite it being three miles away and wearing stiletto court shoes.[17]

Before this, though, my older siblings are also at school and, unwillingly, it is my father who takes us there. Every morning he appears up the road, at the garden gate, revving his engine uproariously and possibly honking the horn if he's getting very impatient. He hates to do this job and, boy, by the red popping veins on his neck, it shows.

One day at my first school, he was so angry that I got ready to jump out of the car as soon as we approached the pavement (SAS commando style if necessary: drop and roll). I was in the front seat and had slightly opened the car door to speed my exit whilst the car was still moving. I was clinging onto it so that it couldn't open any further and I prepared to jump down as he pulled toward the pavement.

Giving him the benefit of the doubt, perhaps he was afraid I would hurt myself (or the car door), but he went 'ballistic'. He slapped me so hard round my face whilst shouting abuse at me that I – completely shocked – went into my first school crying. I was so embarrassed and ashamed that I hid in amongst the coats and shoe-bags in the cloakroom for the morning, not wanting any of my teachers to see me. I was four.

## Self-soothing

*Comfort, comfort my people.*

*Isaiah 40:1*

I was at a friend's wedding. It was idyllic, a beautiful summer's day in a tiny country village church. Then something strange happened. A young, miserable-looking family arrived at the back of the church, near to where I was sitting. Mum held the little boy's hand and Dad had his young four-year-old daughter in his arms. But there was something wrong.

The little girl had obviously been crying, and from the redness of her face and the way her breath was still hiccupping in her body, she had been beside herself. I couldn't tell what the cause had been but I could see that for her it had been genuinely traumatic. She was doing something

---

[17] I still have the corns to prove it!

unusual though; her father wasn't looking at her or talking to her but she was talking to herself. As he walked, she kept saying, 'It will be alright. You are OK now; everything will be fine.' She was only tiny but she was trying to calm herself down, to self-soothe.

The sight of this poor little mite immediately triggered a memory that I had shut out for many years. I remembered that after Dad's violence I would shut myself away, somewhere 'safe' (often in the garden or some fields we lived nearby). I would then pretend that I was outside of myself, looking after upset 'me'. I would say reassuring and comforting things to myself: 'You're going to be OK. It's alright now. You're safe; he can't get you here.' Even though I knew it was me comforting myself, it still seemed to have an effect; my breathing would eventually slow and I would stop hiccupping for breath.

## A teacher's suspicion

I don't know if any of my teachers at St John's first school suspected all was not bliss at home. However, I do remember being about five and having to meet my mum in the headmistress' office during a school day.

I am told by mum the day before that I must have a 'little medical' and when I ask why, she tells me that all the children are having it done. We arrive in the hall with the pretty fish tank; there are no other children having the 'medical'.

The 'medical' seems to involve removing my tights because I remember it being winter and my mum putting them onto the radiator to keep warm, whilst I am looked at by the headmistress in front of my mother. There is no explanation to me, no medical people are involved, no other children seem to be having it done and nothing seems to come of it – so what was that all about?

I would love to be able to say that my mum would have told me the complete truth; sadly, I can't. Did the school suspect something? Remember that this was before the days of the term 'abuse' being widely, if at all, verbalised. I will probably never know. But perhaps being saved was sometimes closer than it seemed at times?

## The winner

My father hates to be beaten at anything. He will win any game at any cost, no matter how small or young I am (or any other contenders, for that matter). I remember once playing water polo at the local swimming pool with some boys; I was about nine. (My dad had, of course, been a county water polo champion.)

I was on the same side as some of the boys and on the opposing team to him. By pure fluke (I don't own any sporting prowess), I had managed to get the ball and was about to pass it. Suddenly, I started to sink under the water, being pulled down by my legs. I shrieked, scared because something or someone seemed intent on drowning me, and as my head was pulled under the water, I of course let go of the ball.

As I tried to battle to the surface, a large sausage hand clomped down onto my head and I was once again thrust under. The hand kept me below the surface (despite my being a strong swimmer). I panicked, scared and unable to breathe. Eventually I got away, and as I came up out of the water I saw – yes, you've guessed it – my father with the ball, shooting for a goal. He is playing against nine-year-olds and his own daughter, but he still *must win.*

## Behind closed doors

Have you ever heard the saying that 'no one knows what goes on behind closed doors'? In other words, we may think we know what a family or home is like but actually only the people behind the doors of a house know the reality.

This saying is not used so widely now, perhaps because abuse *is* becoming more known and spoken about. Back then, abuse was the dirty little secret that was only known by the family who were involved.

My mum noted in her diary that although she had tried to hide her black eye (Dad used to hit her until their children came along) that her neighbour had noticed it but said nothing. It's hard to imagine it now but abuse carried so much shame and guilt (always on the innocent's side) that it was very hard to admit too.

I grew up in a strange world of believing, as a very young child, that everyone got beaten up regularly and that was how all men behaved. Then, when I later found out that my friend's dads didn't beat them up and that some of them were even sweet or gentle to their daughters, I remember being so horrified at my dad's behaviour that I was too ashamed and embarrassed to mention it to friends or family.

Also, in those days (the 60s and 70s) there really was nowhere to go and no one with any power or authority to tell. I believe that if Childline hadn't been invented I would have done it myself, as I know how important it is that children in these situations have a safe and understanding place to go to or even just people to talk to.

## Gravel survival

It's about half past five and the last children's programme of the afternoon is being shown. I'll go up to my room before the boring news comes on and he comes home.

In my room I hear the car drive past the house and into the garage. *Listen!* I can tell by the way he treads on the gravel around our house what sort of mood he's in. It's survival time. A light-footed approach and he'll be smiles, or at least civil. A heavy, foreboding, crushing tread and they'll be venomous words, palpable anger at my very presence and a possible outburst of volcanic proportions that will send me or my siblings flying across the room – and not in a good way.

Life during my childhood was just that: life, otherwise known as survival. *Today might be the day I die; it might be the day my siblings die.* It honestly felt that there was no way to tell who would be alive or dead by the end of it.

I went for a nursing interview when I was sixteen in Exeter. The interviewers asked me:

'What is your greatest achievement in your life?'

I thought for a few seconds.

'Surviving!'

I stated it matter-of-factly but very seriously. They looked a little horrified and were speechless, but actually it felt completely true.

## Divide and conquer

> *For God does not show favouritism.*
>
> *Romans 2:11*

I adore my big sister. She is beautiful and clever, lively and interesting. She has big, beautiful blue eyes (unlike mine), a tall, slim, and statuesque figure (again, unlike mine). She's popular at school (a prefect), good at her studies and very good at art. She's kind to me and lets me hang out with her and her boyfriends (probably much to their annoyance) when she's older. We go out in their cars and I sit silently in the back, on my best behaviour, trying not to be a nuisance, as I love going out with her.

Having researched extensively about abusers, I now understand that they often work on an ancient war philosophy of 'divide and conquer'. A family that is tied tightly together has a lot more power in it with which to overthrow the dictator, so it's in his interest to keep divides wide. One of the ways in which he does this is to 'compare and contrast' his children. He nearly always has a favourite too, as what could be more divisive then pitting them against each other?

My dad has chosen his favourite to aid his plan of divide and conquer and it is my beautiful sister, his literal blue-eyed girl. Don't get me wrong, she receives a regular 'bashing' just like the rest of her siblings, but being favourite does have its compensations and makes his abuse more confusing for me.

In fact, because we're both girls I notice how he treats her differently. I'm the youngest and mealtimes (even when he's being friendly) can be very loud. We all talk a lot and I have to really shout to be heard above the four older voices. However, a curious thing happens; I can have an opinion and I'll tell my dad it and he responds by completely ignoring me, as if I didn't exist. A few minutes later my sister will share the same opinion and my dad not only will listen to her but also praise her for it. I become confused! *Hang on a minute, didn't I just say the very same thing?*

He is also subtly kinder and more respectful to her than to me. When she gets poorly, not always but sometimes presents or Lucozade appear (much to the surprise of my brother and me). When I get poorly, I get shouted at and threatened. One time I had chicken pox and I was so glad to be off school (on account of a bully teacher) that I was in bed, but I was singing. For some reason this annoyed Dad and he shouted up the stairs that he'd come and give me something to cry about if I didn't shut up. 'I thought you were meant to be ill!'

There are countless ways, some subtle and some not so, in which he treats her differently, but they have a profound and lasting effect. Although it doesn't shut me up, I realise that respect from my father and the same kind of love that he has for my sister is an unobtainable thing for me.

As further evidence of divide and conquer, he sets my poor brother up as the absolute scapegoat of the family. Jon gets even more physical abuse than either of his sisters. At times I look back and I genuinely don't know how he wasn't killed.

The effects from Dad's war philosophies amongst the siblings are deep and lasting. We share a sad history, but nonetheless our strength is that we can act as each other's witnesses to the atrocities that went on, and no one can take that away from us.

## Locked out

*I have heard the cries of my people.*

Exodus 3:9

*'My father's a murderer!'*
I'm screaming this out at the top of my lungs.

I have no idea who will hear me but I want – no, *need* – to do *something*. We live in the countryside. All our neighbours are quite far away, so there are no witnesses. There's no one to even tut or shout back, no one to rescue me or stop the savagery. Somewhere a cow may have raised its head or a bird flapping past might have squawked at me, but somehow I doubt it. I am all alone and my maniac father is in one of his blind furies. He's tried to hit me, but I've managed to get away and run outside. However, he has once again locked me out of the house and my fear is that he will now 'go' for my mother; hence the shouting.

I'm not sure what awful crime I have committed this time. It doesn't matter really, not to him; any behaviour that he doesn't deem acceptable at that given moment is his reason (though I call it an excuse). The truth is that he will pick on anything he likes in order to create an argument.

I say an 'argument'; it's more like the depths of hell have opened and fire and brimstone hail out of his mouth and course through his body. His very pores exude violence. His very presence can intimidate. He is a cornered bull of a man, enraged and intent on searing everything in his path to death.

His body-type doesn't help us, his victims. He is a six-foot-two, sixteen-stone hulk of ex-rugby playing brick outhouse – Goliath on steroids (not that he took steroids, he hadn't needed to, he'd been in the Navy) – and I can tell you from personal experience that when you punch that stomach with all your aged-nine-girl might, his muscles are sheer rock!

It's impossible to get back in as all the doors are locked. I run away to some nearby fields and wait and pray that my mum will still be alive when I get back home.

## Family man

Whenever Mum's relatives come to visit there is always a slightly dangerous atmosphere lurking. He's not so bad with my nan because he seems to have charmed her out of being a threat (plus, I don't think she has any idea of his true nature). However, when my lovely Uncle Leslie (Mum's brother) visits, it's a different story. There's a sort of pent-up stiffness about Dad. It's as if he'd love to 'blow' but knows he can't. I wonder if the self-control nearly kills him? There always seems to follow another tempestuous episode once the relatives have left.

## Bullies

> *...everyone should be quick to listen, slow to speak and slow to become angry, for man's anger does not bring about the righteous life that God desires.*
>
> *James 1:19,20*

As I previously mentioned, I was shocked when I found out that my friends' fathers never hit them. Imagine that! *How wonderful,* I thought. Of course, once realisation set in that Dad didn't have to act this way, my loathing for him grew much stronger. *How dare he? How dare he use violence against those whom he is closest to? How dare we let him?* I tried my best to stop him many times. I would stand up against him. I would rail, swearing and shouting just as much as he did; fire against fire, that was my strategy.

The rest of my family, due to their enormous fear of him, would sometimes back away from the confrontation.

'Don't do that, Ali!'

'Don't say that, Alison!'

My mum and older brother and sister would advise me with horror in their voices and in the belief that it would only wind him up more.

Of course, they were right; often I knew I would get hit harder by doing this and that his anger would grow still further. However, to me it was worth it, just to have my say. For some reason I thought it was my job (despite being the youngest and littlest) to protect the rest of my family. It became my identity. I reasoned, *someone's got to stand up to him, and if no one else is willing to take the job on then I'll have to or else we'll all be killed!*

I also believed back then that bullies only understand one language: their own. Therefore, unfortunately, you have to treat them the same way they treat you; reason and logic has no place to these people. I also knew that, bizarrely, although my father's hatred of me was being fed, so was his respect. I might lose countless battles, and painfully too, but eventually I would win the war. *Even then, I believed my father had met his match.*

## Denial

> *You who practise deceit, your tongue plots destruction; it is like a sharpened razor. You love evil rather than good, falsehood rather than speaking the truth.*
>
> *Psalm 52:2-3*

Denial is big business in our house. My father denies that he is less than perfect or that he is to blame for any wrong behaviour. Unfortunately, my mother supports this wholeheartedly. The result is that it can honestly make you go insane unless you keep an iron-vice grip on reality.[18]

So many times, my dad would be in a 'bad mood' and in my instinct to survive I would ask Mum what was wrong with him. My logic was that perhaps I could pre-empt an argument by apologising before he'd lost his temper.

*Every time* she would reply, 'I don't know what you mean, dear. He's not cross. *It must be your imagination...*' (Not once in all my life did she immediately admit it.)

How could it be my imagination?

She would even say it after one of his huge violent outbursts. I would ask, 'Why is Dad angry with me?'

'He's not angry, dear. What are you talking about?'

I would stare in disbelief and utter confusion at her. My mum was a bright lady and normally honest, so this denial was absolutely shocking and it bred in me a hatred of lies and deceit in people. I could never let her get away with it because to do so would be colluding with the denials

---

[18] Psychologists call this term 'gas-lighting' after a reference to an old film in which a husband tries to drive his wife insane by telling her that what she's observing as reality isn't true.

and lies and that would mean that I really *was* going insane. Therefore, I always brought it back to truth, albeit a little sarcastically:

'Well, Mum, if he's not angry with me then why has he just smacked my head against the side of the wall?'

She'd still counter with denial but at least I'd spoken the truth out aloud. To tell someone that something real is their imagination is seriously disturbing to their psyche, especially when they are growing up. How can they ever then trust their own feelings or judgement or even what reality is?

## Sexual tension

> *The Lord detests men of perverse heart but he delights in those whose ways are blameless.*
>
> Proverbs 11:20

My sister and I can't remember Dad sexually abusing us and yet there was always a sense of sexual overlay in his manner toward us. This is sometimes known as 'emotional incest'.[19] For example, the abusive names he called us often had a sexual nature: whore, slut, and so on.

I can't remember definite sexual abuse, thankfully, yet certain times stay with me. I remember that he began a habit of coming into the bathroom whilst my mum was bathing me. I was very small, about four, and I loved bath times because my mum and I would sing together. I clearly remember her unease and that she started to lock the door (the only room that was allowed a lock on) after some of these interruptions.

Another time, when I was a teenager, he drove home drunk from meeting his friends. I was serving him (of course!) his dinner at the table whilst my mother cooked. It was late, so I had on my nightdress. He was in a jolly (half-cut) mood and stuck his hand up inside it to touch my bottom. Thankfully, that time my mother stepped in and stopped him by just shooing me away, but she never addressed it with me. It was just accepted that that was what Dad was like.

## Daydreamer

How do I survive my childhood? I live in a complete fantasy land. The fantasy helps me to escape not just the pain and strife but also the

---

[19] Engel, Beverley; *The emotionally abusive relationship*

loneliness and grief. I have invisible friends, invisible horses, I live in an invisible castle with invisible animals, all is good. There is no fear, no violence, no loneliness. My infant school teacher tells my mum that I have the most vivid imagination of any child she's ever taught. I'm not sure if my mum thinks that is a good thing but to me it is what allows survival and allows it happily.

However, as an adult it is hard to give up this land. Why on earth would I want to live in the real world when my own is so much more exciting? Why, I can be up to Pluto for a spin around the stars and back to the moon to have dinner with that hunky astronaut I met on Jupiter! Who wants to change that? The only trouble with living here though is that nothing real happens. I have to surrender this land when I become a Christian. Not that God is against imaginations – after all, He created them – but I believe He created them for a specific use and it is not to permanently escape reality, which He also created.

I have to surrender fantasy and re-learn what it is like to be totally in reality all the time. It is a hard swop and takes a lot of getting used to. However, eventually I do, and my own real life becomes so much more exciting; I am continually surprised by being more 'present' than I have ever been.

## The protector

Dad wasn't always harmful. Sometimes he would protect me. Once when I was little and we were on holiday, an Alsatian guard dog tried to attack me. It was chained up but its chain was so long that I had mistakenly wandered into its territory. I froze as it jumped at me and tried to bite. Within seconds my dad had got hold of me and pulled me to himself; he shielded me from the dog by putting his arm in the way and the dog tried to bite him.

How sad that his instinct was to protect me from outside harm and yet his inside harm did so much more damage; he couldn't protect me from that – or perhaps didn't want to?

## I'm going to kill him

*An angry man stirs up dissension, and a hot tempered one commits many sins.*

*Proverbs 29:22*

'Right! That's it! I've had enough! I'm going to kill him!'

My brother and I are at home (my sister has left home by this time). We are approximately seventeen and nine years old respectively. Dad has pushed us to the point of beyond exasperation. I can't remember whether he has yet again beaten up my brother (he picks on him most of all of us – the male bear ripping to shreds any male competition, son or not) or whether it has been my turn. Either way, I've had enough!

My brother calmly follows me as I march into the kitchen, grab at the handle of the cutlery drawer and survey the contents. I'm looking for the *big* bread knife.

This is it. This time I really have had enough. We are trapped; Mum won't leave him, there's no one in authority to turn to and I'm desperate! I may look like a long-tangled-haired, vest-protruding, tracksuit-wearing tomboy but inside I'm at least a feisty Charlie's Angel or at most a justice-fighting Wonder Woman!

I grab the knife and seriously consider how I can do this, despite Dad being a brick outhouse of a man and me not quite five-foot-four at this age. I decide I'm probably going to get hurt in this fracas, if not die, but... 'bog' that for a mug of cocoa, it's worth it!

My brother steps in with the voice of reason. He looks out of his NHS black-rimmed glasses and states, 'You can't kill him.'

'I f***ing well can!' (I swear a lot even at this age because I've had the best role model for a child: a parent who does the same.)

He looks at me in a knowing way. 'You can't. *You'll go to prison!*'

I halt. There's a big old institutional fly in my otherwise perfectly planned ointment and it is called 'prison'. *Bummer!* In my blind fury I had forgotten that!

I unwillingly slide the knife back into the drawer. Dad has escaped any consequence for his actions yet again. Where is the justice, Wonder Woman?

## My mum

*Though my father and mother desert me, the Lord will receive me.*

*Psalm 27:10*

I loved my mum; she was a little blonde, blue-eyed cherub of a lady. Others described her as a motherly, gentle, kind and clever lady, and she was. We were always quite close, and I counted her as a best friend as well as a mother. We shared a history of being the youngest in our families, we enjoyed the countryside and books, and I loved her dry sense of humour.

Although she had many virtues, she was not without her vices (like every one of us). For me, her biggest vice was her inability to do that most basic instinct of motherhood: to protect her own.

She made a partial effort at times to stop my dad mid-tantrums. She tried by playing a form of peacemaker, or by asking him to stop – like that was going to happen… – or even occasionally by physically trying to pull him off us when he was attacking us. Of course, all of this was completely ineffectual.

My siblings and I would beg her to leave him. 'Please, get a divorce. Please!'

But she refused.

Sometimes my brother and I would ask if we could go and live at the local orphanage in the town, called 'Pippins'. Anywhere seemed better to us than at home.

We've wondered many times why she wouldn't leave him. It seems she did love him in a perverse sort of way. However, she also seemed to have some sort of block about what was happening to us. I made a counsellor of mine once 'get shivers' down her back when I told her about two things that my mum had done.

Firstly, I'd read a statement in my mum's diary after she had died. She'd written, 'Of course, if Tony [my dad] had treated me the way he treated the children I would have left him a long time ago.'

The second thing was that when I was small and it was bath-time, my mum would sit by the bath and sing to me. I loved these times. My favourite was by the Carpenters: 'Why do stars fall out of the sky?' But she would also try to sing a certain song that really caused me pain and I repeatedly had to ask her not too. The lyrics were, 'Oh, you are a mucky kid, as dirty as the dustbin lid, and when he sees the things that you did, you'll get a-belting from your Pa.' That song would cause me so much pain, even as a tiny child. I just couldn't see how she couldn't connect the song's lyrics with my dad. If she started to sing it, I would beg her to stop.

## Comfort eating

> *The sorrows for the appointed feasts I will remove from you;*
> *they are a burden and a reproach to you.*
>
> *Zephaniah 3:18*

I'm about ten. My brother and sister have left home and any laughter or joy has walked out of the door with them. I miss them very much and I'm lonely. To add to my hopelessness, what was shared between three (the beatings) has now fallen onto one. I'm the only one left so I'm the one Dad picks on.

I work out fairly quickly that when Dad hits me on bone it's far more painful than when he hits me on my flesh. Therefore, I reason, the more flesh I have, the less his beating will physically hurt.

So, I intentionally start to pile on weight, as a protection, by eating whatever sweet thing I can get my hands on. Fat is a major defence mechanism and, in some ways, quite effective. The physical pain lessens but the psychological pain is just beginning.

I don't want to sound like a bad blues song, but I have another source of grief enter my life at about the same time. I have a new teacher; she's sad and bitter and makes everyone in the class cry, including the boys. Suddenly, school, the only other place for me that is safe (besides my grandma and grandpa's house), becomes a place of pain just like home, with its own bully in residence who holds all the power.

Life is bitter and I *long* for some sweetness. I increase my comfort eating – anything sweet I can get my hands on: chocolate, biscuits, cakes, sweets, ice-cream. By age eleven I am eleven stone.

However, this protection is a bitter pill to swallow. I am now one of the fattest girls in school and start to be bullied. Girls pick on me and boys that were once friends (I am a tomboy) become enemies and the name-calling starts:

'Hey, Fatty Boom Boom!'

'Oi, Fatso!'

'It's not Alibaba! It's Ali-blubber!'

'Can you fit through that doorway?'

This compounds the names that I get called at home by my dad. Certain members of my family now also like to comment on my weight-gain. An aunt (who was a model) 'comforts' me one day at the beach by saying, 'Us fatties will sit here.' My nan buys me Maltesers 'as they're not as fattening as normal chocolates'. My mother (who has her own weight issues and self-loathing) despairs that I have inherited her figure. She compares me to my much taller and slimmer sister and I literally 'come up short' and dumpy. When my siblings visit home, their friends start to also comment on my weight and my looks. They probably think that I'm fair game, being little sister, and are doing it just to tease – but it hurts, with that kind of broken heart pain.

All of the verbal abuse and bullying takes its toll and I end up with an eating disorder.

Years later, in my twenties, I meet one of my sister's ex-boyfriends. I am now heading toward anorexia. I weigh about seven-and-a-half stone, at least two stone underweight. I'm completely flat-chested, every rib-bone sticks out, I have dark hollows under my eyes and I'm permanently cold and tired. My sister tries to comfort me by stating, 'You see, I always knew that there was a thin person inside you trying to get out!' Her ex has known me since I was about eight and so has seen me at my heaviest.

'God! You've lost weight!' he exclaims as I answer the door.

'Well, I don't think I was *that* fat!' I try to defend myself.

He looks shocked. 'Fat? No, not really. More like *obese!*'

Somehow that original abuse from Dad has caused me to have an Achilles heel that the enemy, through people, has loved to exploit. Even to this day I can guarantee that I will receive some derogatory comments about my appearance and particularly my weight every few months. It will come through work colleagues, family, friends, church associates and even strangers. For example, 'You're more the deep-fried Mars Bar kind of girl, Alison, aren't you?' 'God, you've put on weight!' 'Two of those people would make up one of you!' 'Can you fit on that pavement?' 'Do you struggle with your weight?' 'Won't you get stuck between those two filing cabinets?' 'Your arse is huge!'

My self-esteem continues to drop, weighed down by this heavy noose around my neck of verbal comments about my appearance. Effects of abuse can last a lifetime.

# CHAPTER THREE

# Bad Hair Day

*Do not make friends with a hot-tempered man, do not associate with one easily angered, or you may learn his ways and get yourself ensnared.*

*Proverbs 22:24-25*

I'm thirteen and I've just had a massive fight with Dad. He's hateful toward me and I equally hate him. I am so angry and frustrated that I want to do something to get my revenge. I go into the bathroom and take the scissors.

'This'll show him!' I mistakenly think.

I take a piece of my long, long hair and begin to cut. Higher and higher I go with the scissors, fuelled by rage and pent-up frustration. How dare he speak to me like that! *Snip!* How dare he treat me like that! *Snip!*

Of course, I'm cutting off my nose – or rather my hair – to spite my face, but that won't occur to me until after the weekend and I have to go to face people at school. All I can think of right now is revenge, and because I can't mete it out on Dad, it has to be turned inward against myself. Once I've finished, my hair resembles a monk-style haircut up around my ears, the shortest I've had it since I was five. There – that will show him!

At dinner time I sit at the table in our kitchen, minus fifteen inches of beautiful Barnet[20]. And my father? He doesn't even notice.

---

[20] hair

## Too sensitive

I am constantly told that I am 'too sensitive', by Dad but more ironically by Mum when she's explaining Dad's behaviour to me: 'Don't be so silly! Don't take it to heart! He didn't mean it! He didn't do that! He didn't say it like that!'

This strikes me as strange. Surely sensitivity is a good characteristic to have? It makes you kind and compassionate, able to empathise and be of support to people. Surely it is better than its opposite, complete insensitivity – like Dad, who is as sensitive as a brick. He seems to have no ability to feel another's pain, no ability to see another's side or respect their character. Only his pain matters or is even real to him.

I am also constantly told by Dad, 'You're weird!' It's one of his favourites for me. It's not as abhorrent as the sexual name-calling when he's in full blown tantrum. It's just one that he saves for me when things are calmer.

'Weird': the dictionary[21] says it means, 'strange, unnatural, un-normal, unearthly, eerie'. It's an unusual put-down, but an effective one for a daughter. It makes me think, 'There must be something abnormal about me; I'm not like everyone else. I'm unnatural, not even earthly; I'm shocking.' Down tumbles my self-worth once again. In addition to all the things he says I am, now I am not even worthy of living on the earth. My reactions (usually to his bad behaviour) must be abnormal and not trustworthy.

Of course, it's all b***. He knows full well that my reactions to his inappropriate behaviour – namely anger, a sense of injustice, not accepting, not negotiating – are all valid, completely normal and appropriate. It is *he* who is 'weird', his sense of power and dominion that is unearthly, his anger and vileness that are unnatural. Why on earth would you want to control your whole family, and why use fear and intimidation to do it? How is that love?

It is the look in his eyes that at times appears eerie. He has a killer's stare and it is his seemingly absolute lack of self-control that invokes shock in us all.

---

[21] Collins English Dictionary (online)

## Penny-pincher

I got a weekend job at fourteen so that I could become more independent. I worked Saturday and Sunday cleaning in *The Rising Sun* pub and working in the kitchens washing up, earning what seemed a fortune to me compared to my pocket money. I bought all my own clothes and any other necessities that I needed, but my parents still paid for my housing and food.

My dad charged me for my phone bills and I had to make an account of how long each call had lasted. I had started to go out with a lad who had moved away to university so calls became more frequent (though I would ask him to ring me as much as possible). One day Dad started to shout abuse at me about how much I was on the phone (despite me making an honest list of the timings). We had a row and I said I would pay for however much it was.

When the bill came through he totalled the time and told me how much I had to pay and by when. (It was a large amount and not all mine!) I gathered all my savings from my weekend work and all the pennies I had left over and gave it to him. Later he came roaring, shouting and swearing at me. As he had *all* my savings, I couldn't think of what could be wrong.

'You're two b****y pence short!' was the explanation I was given.

I stared in disbelief. How mean was that? I'd given all I had and it wasn't even as if I was costing them a huge amount anyway. How mean could he get, for the sake of two pence? I later found a two-pence piece and went storming into his office at home (as usual fighting fire with fire).

'Here's your ****** two-pence piece, you mean ******!' I shouted it as I flung it across his desk at him.

'Thank you!' he sneered sarcastically, pleased with himself that he'd got his way again.

## The Violent Dream

> *A gentle answer turns away wrath, but a harsh word stirs up anger.*
>
> *Proverb 15:1*

I have a recurring dream as I grow up. My dad is once again going on and on at me. He's in my face, shouting, swearing, telling me how despicable I am and how worthless. I snap, and I seem to be empowered with an incredible human strength (Wonder woman, eat your heart out!) As this strength fills me to overflowing, I grab my six-foot-two father by the throat and I lift him up off his feet. (I don't know the mechanics of how this can happen because I'm far too short to do this in reality, but hey, it's my fantasy and I can do what I like!) I place him up against a brick wall.

I explain to him in a low menacing growl how I am not happy with his behaviour and there will be consequences if he does it again. He is unable to hit out or kick and has to listen to me, his feet still dangling and getting just a little taste of how powerless he makes us all feel. Then I let him drop and walk on my merry way. There is no kick back and I feel empowered at last.

I imagine I am the only one to have such a strange fantasy of domestic life until I read a reassuring psychology book that explains that this is perfectly normal for victims of abuse. *Phew!* I'm not such a weirdo after all!

## Laughter as medicine

> *For the Lord laughs at the wicked.*
>
> *Psalm 37:13*

Laughter is the saviour in our house. It probably seems that there wasn't a lot of joy or happiness from what you have read so far, but in fact we do laugh (although, true, it's usually when Dad isn't around).

I don't know quite how we manage to make jokes out of the obscenity that is Dad's moods, but somehow we do, and somehow it makes it more bearable. There is a sort of madness about him and his paranoia that does contain black humour.

One afternoon my sister and I are sat talking, when our dad comes in and starts pointing at me:

'You've broken the b****y toilet lid and you've done it by banging it down too hard when you've finished!'

I'm genuinely shocked and can't remember breaking the lid – and besides, wouldn't I have noticed? I go to look at what he's trying to mend. A pipe that runs around the bathroom is leaking four feet away from the toilet. It bears no relation to the lid at all.

I'm not accepting this accusation; I reply, 'Well, if you didn't keep leaving the toilet lid up, I wouldn't have to bang it down!' Touché, mister, stick that in your pipe (so to speak) and smoke it.

I come back to tell my sister the hideous thing I've done breaking the 'lid' and we dissolve (albeit quietly in case he hears) into fits of giggles.

I once saw the screenwriter and actor Mel Brooks being interviewed about his musical *The Producers*. He was asked, as he was Jewish, how he could laugh and make jokes about Hitler and the Holocaust. He said that the quickest way to remove the threat of the enemy is to bring them down to size, and what better way to do that than to laugh at them. I guess we do the same with dad.

# CHAPTER FOUR

# Sweet Talker

*For whoever touches you, touches the apple of his eye.*
*Zechariah 2:8*

I am in my twenties and in a serious relationship with a lovely man of the same age. One afternoon, we meet up with all my family in a café for a cup of tea, and as I sit next to him, he naturally has his arm around my shoulders. But when I get home, my father goes through the roof, becoming extremely aggressive and shouting abusively at me, saying how disgusting I am for 'fondling' my boyfriend in public.

On another occasion, that same boyfriend calls round to my house and we spend time up in my bedroom, innocently chatting. I can hear my dad arguing with my mum downstairs and, sure enough, after he's slammed the doors, my mum calls up to me. I came to the top of the stairs and she looks upset.

'Your dad says, can you both come down here rather than be alone in your room?'

I am livid, just at the ludicrous idea of it all. Why on earth, if we were going to have sex, would we do it in my bedroom with my dad around? Also, what sort of a coward is he that he sends my mum to do his dirty work?

I shout back, 'This is ridiculous, Mum! You know that we're just chatting! If it so bothers him, why can't he come and tell me to my face?'

With that, the kitchen door is flung open. He's obviously been listening. He tosses Mum out of the way and starts to walk slowly but menacingly up the stairs toward me, pure hatred in his eyes.

'Listen to me, you b****! I make the b****y rules in this house, not you! And if I say, get out of your room, you *will* get out! Understand? You're a despicable wh***!'

Unperturbed, I shout back, 'How sad are you? You've such a sick mind that you can't even believe that two friends can just be chatting!'

As I rail on, he makes his way up toward me and I back toward my bedroom. However, something odd then happens. As he makes his way toward me, I can see a thought flicker across his mind and he stops. This is highly unusual, as without doubt he would usually have gone for me[22] by now.

I then realise that he had suddenly remembered that I am not alone, that my boyfriend (also over six foot) is sitting in my room, listening to all of this. Dad suddenly swerves off his course of coming after me and goes into his own room, still shouting and swearing but no longer a violent threat.

The funny truth of the matter is that my boyfriend is beautiful and gentle and hates violence. He wouldn't hurt a fly, but my Dad doesn't know that and as he judges by his own standards, he saw him as a threat. As with all bullies, he is ultimately a coward.

## The babe magnet

> *People look at the outward appearance, but the Lord looks at the heart.*
>
> *1 Samuel 16:7 (TNIV)*

Women flock to my dad. True, he was handsome as a young man and very athletic and virile. However, even since he prematurely went bald in his thirties – much to his horror – women have still adored him. (He is like a toupee-less Sean Connery!) I see women flirting with him all the time. He has some sort of animal magnetism that the poor, senseless creatures get drawn into, much to my repulsed and confused horror. 'Can't you see what he's really like?' I think. 'Can't you see it's all a charm act?'

I'm not quite sure whether he had affairs or not. Of course, he swears not to my mum but her diaries record stories of him flirting and staying out late with work colleagues' wives. She was also understandably jealous so it is hard to know the truth of their youth.

---

[22] attacked me

Later, when she is slowly dying of cancer and my dad is meant to be 'nursing' her, he is actually writing to a woman who openly becomes his girlfriend once she has died.

A few years later when he becomes very poorly himself and is at his nursing home, my father has a selection of what can only be described as... well... groupies. This group of female carers tell me how fond they are of him and how lovely he is, how lucky I am to have a father like that! Even on his deathbed in hospital, my sister and I walk in on this group of admiring nurses from his nursing home, all surrounding him. Much to our utter amazement, they are standing over him cooing their admiration, attending to him, rubbing his face and reassuring him.

'Poor Tony! It'll all be OK,' they whisper.

My sister and I are shocked and a little horrified. He is quite poorly and barely conscious at this point, but I could swear he has a satisfied, almost smug smile on his face, loving all the attention as usual!

## Nightmares

*I will lie down and sleep in peace, for you alone, O LORD, make me dwell in safety.*

*Psalm 4:8*

I frequently have nightmares as a child that will go on into my thirties. My nightmares often consist of two recurrent themes. One is an enormous tidal wave that I see roaring up toward me. I know it will crash over me and kill me and there isn't anything I can do about it.

The other theme is of being with someone who looks identical to someone I know well or am related too. However, although they look the same, it isn't them but someone else in disguise, who turns on me and tries to kill me. I run and run, and they chase and chase until they track me down.

I know that these nightmares relate to Dad. It isn't until after many years of healing and prayer that they stop. But eventually they do stop.

## She's leaving home

*...a time to plant and a time to uproot...*

*Ecclesiastes 3:2*

The day I officially leave home is very stressful for me. It should be a day of sadness at the thought of leaving (if home life has been happy) mixed with excitement at the start of a new adventure. However, Dad makes sure it is neither.

It is as if he realises that he will no longer have any control over me and is not happy about it! To leave his last personal stamp, he starts an almighty argument as I literally pack my stuff up.

I am going off to do my nursing training and have managed to fit all my household possessions that I will need (e.g. kettle, duvet, pillows and clothes) into six bin bags! There is just one problem: I drive an old Mini! Far from feeling worried about this, I lay everything out on the landing to work out how I will fit it all in.

Dad goes ballistic! 'You can't leave all your cr** here! What do you think you're doing?' *Well, Dad, I'm climbing the Eiffel Tower!* It's pretty obvious what I'm doing so I don't dignify it with an answer. 'That's never going to b****y well fit into your car! Hell's teeth!' and so it goes on and on.

As usual, I try at first to reason with him. 'Don't worry, Dad, I'm not leaving it here, I'm just working out where it will go.' No answer is right; he swears and becomes abusive and absolutely illogical.

In the end, I pack that Mini as quickly as I can, stuffing those bags in like a black crumpled elephant. Never has so much been fitted into so little space so quickly! Mum is crying and I am sad to leave her, but another part of me can't wait to get away.

As I drive through the beautiful countryside to get to the nurses' home, I cry. What a shame! What a shame that all I feel at leaving home is relief and the only sadness I feel is linked to why my dad had to be such a b*****d to me, even as I escaped him. All those years of him trying to get rid of me, and at last the day has come, but in leaving his domain he knows I am also leaving his power.

I drive to the nurses' home through the beautiful hilly countryside; then, a huge rainbow appears over the road. It is the promise of a new start, a sign of hope and a symbol of escape from all of the floods of tears and storms of living with that man.

## Dental problems

> *The truth will out.*
>
> Shakespeare, The Merchant of Venice

Why do dentists ask you a question when the whole of their hand is in your mouth? *What kind of kamikaze profession is this?! Don't you know that if I reply it will involve biting at least a little bit of your finger off? Don't you need fingers to make a living?*

Undeterred, the white coat (not *those* type) continues. 'So, when were you in the car crash?'

Oh no, here we go again! Embarrassment and dread are starting to make me blush.

'I've never been in a car crash,' I answer truthfully.

'Well, you must have been! Your X-rays definitely show the signs of significant trauma to all the upper teeth on your right side. Just look at the way the roots are all curved! It looks as though you've hit the dashboard at speed!'

Not this old chestnut again; this is the third dentist in a row who's spotted the signs of trauma. I sigh but brace myself. 'It's not the result of a car crash. It's where my dad used to hit me in the face.'

Here we go again: the blushing, the startled looks from white coat and his poor innocent nurse, the muteness; what words can they say? Strangely, I have to be the one who has the words of comfort.

'It's OK, it was a long time ago. I've escaped him now. Actually, he's dead so I've really escaped him!'

They look slightly less worried and scared, and as I leave, the nurse kindly hands me some extra samples of mini Colgate and floss. Bless her! It's as if she is trying to make up for my whole row of tooth abscesses and root fillings as a result of the damage to my mouth having been smacked in the face so often. It's sweet and kind of her and reminds you that not all humans are bad.

## Working wonders

*You will praise the name of the Lord your God, who has worked wonders for you.*

*Joel 2:26*

One of the first ways I learnt about God's amazing power in my life was seeing Him work a miracle in my father. I was upstairs in my bedroom and for some reason Dad had decided that I'd done something infinitely wrong (although I can't tell you what it was) and he was on the warpath to tell me so. I heard him roar (literally) at the foot of the stairs, 'Where the **** are you, you despicable madam'? ('Madam' only came out when I was in trouble. At least that was the polite version compared to the usual impolite verbal abuse.)

57

With the shouting came the threatening rumble of him mounting the stairs, all sixteen stone of thundering train-crash power that was about to be let loose on my body.

I had just become a Christian and had been privileged to receive amazing teaching from my church and mentors. This teaching told me that God was able to do anything, that nothing was impossible for Him. 'Well, God, let's put you to the test and see how you handle this one?' I said an urgent yet simple prayer with my new childlike faith: 'Please protect me and do something to him!'

Now, the normal scenario for this type of rage usually saw my father enter my room, grab me, shout some obscenities whilst blaming me for some inane thing, and then start slapping me – or kicking me if I fell to the ground. That was just the way life was, and unless I could escape, there was no way out.

I got to my bedroom door in the hope of somehow running away, but as I did so I looked at Dad as he climbed the stairs and saw a miraculous thing. As he came pelting up, his whole demeanour changed. Away went the pent-up fury that was about to be unleashed, away went the swearing and false accusations, and in its place a calm peacefulness came over him. He was no longer charging forward, hate and venom spitting from his eyes and mouth. He was upright, calm and smiling and (this is the weirdest bit) as he reached the top of the stairs, he put his hand into his pocket and said to me, 'Would you like a wine gum?'

*Would I like a wine gum?!* Oh my gosh, what kind of freaky, out of character behaviour was this? Within seconds God had somehow completely removed my father's rage and had made him turn into sweetness and light.

My dad did normally come out of his black tempers, but it usually took at least a week of silent sulking after one of his blasts, then at least a week of apparent sucking up to his victims. However, this process had taken less than seconds and right before my eyes. Now, *that* is a God who powerfully answers prayer! *Wow!* And if God could change my father like that, well, He could do anything! What a lesson in faith.

(I just have to say, in case any of you are reading this and prayed similar prayers to this but were disappointed with the answers, that my prayers weren't always answered this way. Sometimes it worked and sometimes it didn't, and I don't know why.)

## Wedding day

It is the day of my wedding and the run-up to it has been as per normal weddings: very stressful. My dad has refused to pay for anything to do with it, not because he is not approving of my future husband but because his usual meanness has stepped in. Therefore, my future in-laws have very kindly offered to pay for all the food at the reception and I am paying for everything else with the money that my mum has left me in her will.

It sounds stupid but I am amazed at my dad's meanness. Also, to take the biscuit, it hasn't stopped him inviting nearly twenty of his own friends to the reception. It is all a bit embarrassing for me as I try to explain it to my in-laws, 'My dad won't pay for anything and – oh, by the way, he's got twenty of his friends coming that he'd like you to pay for!' Thankfully, they are generous and full of grace about it and say nothing.

Before the wedding, I try to keep the time that I'm with him to the minimum, therefore I don't arrive with him and instead my bridesmaid's lovely dad drives me to the church.

My dad walks up to the car; he is smiling a tight smile, he sticks his thumb up at me but says nothing about how I look, nor of course gives any reassurance about the day. My heart drops once again. He can't even manage a compliment for my wedding day! He wanders off as soon as I'm out of the car and I go up to speak to my vicar, Peter, who's taking the wedding service, to try to explain 'without explaining' how complex the relationship with Dad is.

'Peter, Dad's not always completely... *reliable!*' Is the only way I can think to put thirty-four years of abuse into subtle wedding-appropriate language!

'What do you mean? Might he not turn up'? Peter looks concerned.

I pause and laugh nervously. 'No, he's here, but things are *tricky.*'

'OK,' Peter reassures me with a smile. 'Well, we'll just wait and see and then play it by ear.'

I relax slightly.

Whether just from this comment Peter had picked up that all was not happy at Camp Reid or whether he had sensed things about Dad from numerous healing services he'd run, I don't know, but he does a clever and healing thing for me in that service. At the point where the service states, 'Who gives this woman?' my dad steps forward: 'I do.' Peter puts my hand into my dad's and then puts it into the hand of my future husband, David, which, I think, is the normal tradition of the Anglican Church. However (and I don't think this is normally in the service) Peter then firmly takes my dad's right hand and his wrist, and gently but firmly pushes him away from my side, to stand behind me.

He whispers to him, 'Your job's done now.' However, it isn't a kind or reassuring whisper but one full of authority and certainty, and possibly even slightly menacing. It is as though he is saying, 'Back off! She's no longer yours; you have no rights over her.'

It sounds a strange thing but I'm sure Peter is doing it intentionally and it is so healing to me. Dad's sense of ownership over me is so strong and here is my kind vicar before the altar of God pushing him away from me and severing his ties. So much so that I giggle nervously in relief and you can see me wink at the vicar in our wedding video – as though I'm saying, *thank you, I know what you're doing!*

Of course, Dad has to have the last word and the final straw comes for me when he starts to insist that all of *his* friends get into the wedding photos (that I am paying for). I make an ungraceful bride shouting at him across the photo line, but what's the use? He gets his way even at our wedding.

## His dream, my power

*A father to the fatherless.*

*Psalm 68:5*

Many years later my father told me of a very vivid dream he had had. In it I was burning down his beloved house that he had built with his own hands. He was astounded and afraid in the dream, and I then realised in a perverse turnaround of power that my father had come to fear me. Although, if I'm really honest, a tiny part of me was quietly pleased that at last he knew what that fear of a relative was like, the majority of me was sad. I didn't want my father to fear me! I wanted him to love me and show me respect, to know his daughter and be pleased with her.

# CHAPTER FIVE

# Mind Games

*Then we will no longer be infants, tossed back and forth by the waves and blown here and there by every wind of teaching and by the cunning and craftiness of men in their deceitful scheming.*

*Ephesians 4:14*

Mind games are the bread and butter of an abuser, and hopefully some of my father's will ring bells so that you can be empowered to realise that:

- you're not alone;
- none of them are your fault;
- your abuser uses these knowingly and willingly in order to dominate you;
- you can escape them.

## Sauce for the goose

To my father, women are for housework, cooking and sex. To be fair to him, he was brought up in an era of male chauvinism. But despite living through the feminist movement of the sixties, his excitement was only stirred because their battle cry of 'burning your bras' meant, well, women going bra-less.

He expects my mother not only to work for him at his office but also to see to all their children's needs and then to cook his dinner for him by the time he gets home. I am appalled at his treatment and become a true child of feminism. I watch *Charlie's Angels* and *Wonder Woman* and – do you know what? – it's worked. Even my own mother states, 'What's sauce for the goose is sauce for the gander.' It's just a pity that she can't live up to the saying. Unfortunately, she accepts his chauvinism and becomes his slave.

As a teenager I talk a lot about feminism around my parents and hint at the behaviour of 'male chauvinist pigs'. His favourite retort is, 'Just you wait, my girl, until you get a man. You'll be waiting on him just like your mother.'

Stuff that for a mug of cocoa! I create an immediate rule for future boyfriends: they must be able to cook and be happy to occasionally do domestic things for me or they're out. Poor lads! So many unknown rules, but luckily I pick well, and males with any sign of chauvinism don't ever arrive at Station Ali.

Just to prove his point, I realise that the first time my dad ever does anything domestic for me is after my mother has died. I go round to his flat and he makes his usual statement, 'Would you like a cup of tea?' This seems polite but is actually code for, 'I want tea, so go and make it.'

I agree and head toward the kitchen, but something bizarre happens; he also gets up. Not only does he get up, but he puts the kettle on and reaches for the tea bags. I don't believe it: *my father is making me a cup of tea!* I sit down in shock, realising that this is the first time ever he's done something domestic for me. I'm thirty-three.

## Disappearing acts

My dad's favourite mind game with me is to offer something that he knows I would like or would be really useful to me. I accept and then he'll either give it to someone else or just deny that he offered it or, worst still, go back on it at the last minute. This is awkward when he's offered a lift and then fails to show up, or you go to collect some chairs he's promised to you and find them strapped to your brother's car instead, or he makes you some shelves having offered to do it for free and you then get a bill for the wood.

Usually, having been brought up with this, I wouldn't dream of asking him for anything or for any help. It would only entail being disappointed or, worse still, being indebted to him, and for that I would have to suffer at his time and convenience. However, sometimes I let my guard slip and stupidly try to trust him again.

My 'favourite' was when he offered to take my car to the garage to be checked over. (I had bought it from my mum when she had had a brain tumour and became too poorly to drive, and she had since died.) When I returned to collect it, strangely it wasn't sitting in the drive. On questioning where it was, he told me that he'd sold it to the garage. I never saw the money or the car again! A word springs to mind and sadly it isn't forgiveness.

## A little slap

My father never apologised to me. He did to my brother and sister but never to me. After my mother had died, he lived alone having been deserted by several girlfriends. He became quite poorly with a very unusual lung condition. He had a carer to go in each day, and if he was very desperate (for example, his commode needed emptying when his carer was away) I would go in to help. However, I refused to nurse him consistently. Not because I couldn't bear to but because, if I'm honest, I was worried that he would still play games with me and be offensive and that I might one day snap and hurt him.

I got a lot of criticism for not 'caring for him more' by his best friend Brian. Of course, he didn't have a clue about the abuse. I'm afraid I felt I had to tell him in order to explain, but *he didn't want to know.* He couldn't bear the fact that his 'lovely' best friend was indeed a wife- and child-beater.

However, Brian did ask my dad about it and my dad then told me. Having faced Dad with the truth about his anger and violence, I now hoped for an apology, but he only said, 'Well, things were different in those days. We all did it. It was only a little slap.'

To this I reminded him about the time when he'd burst into my room when I was about five (I'd woken him up due to my crying because of a nightmare and I was afraid of the dark). He'd literally leapt onto me in my bed, shouting and swearing and shaking me, telling me to stop crying whilst hitting me (logic was never his strong point). My poor teenage brother had witnessed everything and tried to stop him, only to be thrown across the room like a rag doll. (Many years after my dad had died, my brother told me the story from his point of view. He choked back the tears and sadness as he did so; it was heartbreaking to see that this poor young boy had tried to defend his little sister but was obviously no match for a huge, grown man. I loved him for trying though.)

Back to the present, immediately my father went into his own usual self-justifying and obsessed mode. 'God, yes you *would* cry; it was b****y irritating and I needed my sleep!'

An apology never came. I wasn't surprised. In fact, within minutes of this conversation I was looking at some photos with him that I'd brought to show him.

'Who's that?' he asked me, pointing to me in a very clear photo.

'It's me, Dad!' I said incredulously, amazed that he couldn't tell, but I should have known better and been warier.

His only sneering answer was, 'God, you've put on weight!'

He *had* to kick back at me for standing up to him and he used the most effective tool to him, now that he was physically sick and weak. He used verbal abuse, knowing my weakest spot and the area that could do most damage to me: my appearance and weight.

## The seducer

My dad was an excellent seducer, so much so that even now many friends and family have no clue about his real character.

When I was younger, if my friends met him, they would say, 'I wish I had a dad like yours!'

I would be incredulous. 'Do you?' I'd enquire, partly astounded at the thought and yet partly unsurprised as yet again his mastery of charm had duped another.

Now at his funeral my lovely cousin comes up to me and, I'm sure in order to say something comforting, tells me how fond he was of my dad. 'He was my favourite uncle.'

'Was he?' I enquire, knowing that my cousin is only trying to be kind but realise that it's more proof of dad's charm initiative.

'Yes, he was always adventurous and would take me sailing with him or doing sport.'

Obviously, I can't say anything to my cousin as he has no idea of the truth and I don't want to steal his illusion of a favourite boyhood uncle. It's true my dad did have a very adventurous side and he could be great fun, just as long as you had the distance of being a nephew and weren't too connected. How sad that he couldn't have been so kind to his own son.

# CHAPTER SIX

# Paranoia

*He will wipe every tear from their eyes. There will be no more death or mourning or crying or pain, for the old order of things has passed away.*

*Revelation 21:4*

My dad is completely paranoid. Whether it's impossibly impractical window locks to stop burglars (though why they can't smash the windows instead, I never know) or putting gravel around the house (so that you can hear the intruders) or keeping masses of tinned food in a cupboard (in case of nuclear war), his ways are extreme.

Sadly, in the last months of life his paranoia goes into overdrive, or so it seems. My husband and I go to visit him one evening in his nursing home. We sit in the lounge drinking tea.

'Of course, they never lock the b****y patio doors here!'

'Oh Dad, of course they do. I'm sure you don't need to worry about that,' I try to console him.

My husband gets up to show him that he's safe. Unfortunately, as he tugs the huge glass door, the whole thing slides smoothly open! Dad looks at us completely exasperated as though we are mad.

'I told you! And they've put salt in my tea again rather than sugar!'

'Oh Dad, they wouldn't have mixed those up!' I state incredulously.

Again, my husband dips his finger in the sugar bowl.

'It's salt,' he states as a matter of fact.

That's the trouble with crying wolf; no one believes you even when it's true.

Thankfully, this paranoia didn't really seem to affect me when growing up, probably due to it being so illogical. Plus, we didn't need any imagined paranoia about outside forces. We had a real-life threat living and breathing right in our house.

## Trust

When my father became terminally ill, he became hypoxic (lacking oxygen) and this made him confused. (In fact, what it really did was show his true nature; he became aggressive and verbally abusive, much to the shock of the nursing staff whom he had once again fooled into believing that he was a sweet and charming old-timer.)

I was called to try to calm him down. I walked down the corridor to see him leading the poor staff a merry hell. He was shouting and swearing, trying to wheel his wheelchair away down the hall whilst still being attached to the oxygen tubing in his room.

He saw me and shouted down the hall, 'Ah, thank God you've arrived!'

'Dad, do you know me?' I wasn't quite sure of his state of mind, he seemed so addled.

'Yes, of course I ****** do!' He swore at me as usual.

'Do you trust me?'

My nursing training was kicked into gear at the situation. I enquired not because I was sure of the answer but because I knew I was going to have to try to calm him down, and if he didn't have that basic feeling of trust in me then he wasn't going to listen to me.

'Of course, I do!' He looked typically cross and exasperated at my stupidity.

How strange that the man I could never trust or feel safe with felt completely at ease, even safe, with me, now that the tables had turned and he was vulnerable. How sad. What a waste. What a waste of a life and a waste of a father-daughter relationship.

## Funeral director's fear

I was asked a strange question a few days after my father had died at the Funeral Directors'. Two of the funeral directors that had laid out his body called me aside. They appeared a little disturbed but also curious about something.

One of them whispered to me, 'I hope you don't mind me asking you this, but was your dad quite an intimidating man when he was alive?' He looked very worried.

'Yes, you could say that,' I replied, reluctant to give too much information but slightly fascinated at what they would say next.

'We thought so! There was something very scary about him. Even as we laid him out, we agreed that we wouldn't want to have met him on a dark night!'

Even in death there was something sinister about my dad.

## The prospect of peace

After my father had died, my sister and brother-in-law and I went to visit the vicar to sort out the funeral arrangements. It was important to my sister and me that a true picture of my father was given, as we didn't feel we could stomach a wonderfully saintly obituary. Although we wanted to honour him, we wanted to do it in truth rather than to continue the cycle of yet more deceit or denial.

However, when we had discussed this with a beloved relative of ours, he insisted that he didn't want anything negative spoken of Dad at the funeral. This placed us in a dilemma. We loved this relative; he had always been very good to us and because we were so fond of him, we didn't want to upset him.

The vicar, John, asked what sort of man my father was and we all fell silent. Suddenly, my sister said in a very calm but impassioned voice, 'He was a very, very violent man!' John was brilliant; he understood immediately. We then explained that family members didn't want this mentioned and yet my siblings and I, and our spouses, all knew the truth.

On the day of the funeral service, the vicar handled this problem very well. He explained how my father, although a man of creativity and sociability, was also full of 'light and shade' and was 'very complex'. It was enough for us; his good side was acknowledged as was his dark side, be it ever so subtly.

On that same day of sorting out the funeral, John asked if he could pray for us at the end of the meeting. He began with these words: 'We thank you, Lord, for the *prospect of peace.*' As John spoke those three simple words about a coming peace, the truth of them crashed upon my heart, like a massive wave crashing over a pier. A type of hysteria raised itself in my chest and I had to muffle a scream and huge sobs, not of pain but of relief. I couldn't hear anything else he spoke afterwards. It was as if something magnificent had happened in my heart with those words.

You see, my father had always set himself against me (he was against all my family, but I had had those years of living with him on my own, without my siblings, and he saw me particularly as an enemy because I stood up to him). It had been like a never-ending war for the last thirty-eight years (my whole life to date) and I was battle-weary.

What did this battle consist of? Well, obviously there was the violence and verbal abuse, the psychological mind games, the disappointments and lies, denials and put-downs. Thirty-eight years of battle takes its toll. You get world-weary, heavy, burdened and weak. Joy is always shadowed by sadness. Suddenly as John said those words, 'Thank you for the prospect of peace,' it struck me: *I don't have to fight any more!*

A huge weight lifted from me as I realised that never again would I have to be subjected to all manner of atrocities and hurt at the hands of this one man, my father. Never again would I have to be in his presence and force myself to fight back in his arena.

I did grieve for my father. True, it wasn't for the man he was; it was rather for all the man that he could and should have been. It was for all that missed father-daughter relationship; all those occasions when I'd longed for a daddy I could trust, a kind, honest, loving, accepting, gentle, respectful, considerate, humble and patient father. I grieved all those occasions when he was the opposite.

It shocks some people to hear me say this (usually people who have no concept of having lived with an abusive person, let alone a parent) but having grieved for this longed-for father, I had no tears left for my real one. In fact, the only feeling I had was a huge relief.

At that point a deep peace and joy entered my heart and has never left. It was this 'prospect of peace' that suddenly announced a bright and shining glory. Hope had entered my future and joy could visit un-haunted.

I say this because I want you to know that if you have been abused, you too could one day feel this peace and joy. Hopefully it won't take someone's death to help you feel this (though if it does, because your abuser has died or taken his own life, please don't feel guilty; we really do reap what we sow). But you too may know the prospect of peace within your own life one day. It is possible.

## If I had a hammer

It is the day of Dad's funeral. It isn't all that many years since we have buried Mum. When Mum died, I placed some violets – one of her favourite flowers – in with the coffin. My sister and I had wanted Mum to have an ornate and pretty burial stone (one that she would have liked – a little ironically, considering that she was dead and would never see it!) Dad wouldn't hear of it and chose a typically huge, ugly plain stone block as her headstone, with minimal wording.

However, today he is gone and my sister and I can 'go to town'. First of all, we get the call: what clothes do you want him buried in? Now, my dad loved his fashion, as had his father before him. (As I said in chapter 1, my grandpa had been known wearing natty lemon spats on his shoes!) Dad prided himself on the latest fashions, be that the chunky jumpers and beard of the arty 50's or the huge collars and length of sideburns in the 70's.

Now we can seek revenge and – oh, it is sweet! (If you haven't been brought up by an abusive parent or had to suffer abuse in your own life, this act will probably seem very cruel or bitter. If you have, you'll understand completely. It's not that you want the abuser to suffer; it's just a way of expressing that frustration that has never been allowed to be expressed whilst the abuser was present. It's a type of harmless but mischievous expression of feeling. At least, that is our excuse.)

We try to think of something from his wardrobe that is decidedly dodgy and that he can spend all eternity (metaphorically speaking) wearing. *Yahoo!* Dad never played golf, but we hit upon the ugliest pair of tartan trousers you could find this side of a golf-course, let alone eternity.

We laugh (albeit secretly, as only our husbands and brother know about it); revenge is sweet! In fact, I will still have a little smile in the years ahead, whenever I drive up the hill past where he's buried and think of those trousers.

We also buy a new headstone as he is of course going into the same grave as Mum. (He already planned that he would lie on top of Mum for all eternity! Once a dominator, always a dominator. This is such as shame for me as I like to occasionally visit my mum's grave and take flowers. I know she's not there, but it is as though he is still dominating and coming between us.)

However, she who laughs last... My sister produces a beautiful design of angels to be carved on the new stone and I request that a line from one of Mum's favourite poems be put onto it – simple but satisfying ideas that previously have been blocked by Dad.

I also take it a little further. I just need to give you a little of my history to explain this next step. When I did my nurse's training in those days, it really was a general nurse qualification and you did a stint of psychiatric nursing. One day whilst in the psychiatric hospital, I joined in on an art therapy class. The subject was to draw what different family members had meant to you in your life. When we'd finished our pictures, we each had to put them in the middle of the class for all to see. There amidst the psychiatric patient's bright beautiful flowers and butterflies was a stark black-and-white creation with lots of symbols on it.

The therapist looked disturbed and asked nervously, 'Whose is this?'

I hesitantly lifted my hand as the poor, frightened patients eyed me with real suspicion, thinking, 'And *you've* come to look after *us?*'

True, I had included many lovely symbols. My sister and brother were stars and my Grandma had been a heart, but there at the side was a huge hammer.

'Whom does this represent?' the teacher queried.

'It's my father,' I said nonchalantly, trying not to alarm any of the inpatients.

You see, all of my life my father has battered me (mentally, not just physically). He has tried to squash my personality and character, hope, joy, confidence and even the reality out of me. It has been like living under a huge hammer that regularly beats me down into nothingness.

Now that he has died and the 'prospect of peace' has become very real to me, I want to mark the end of his reign of terror over me in a symbolic way. I wonder how I could do this and then have an idea. I tell my husband one evening with only a slight glint of madness in my eyes. 'I want to bury Dad with a hammer!'

My husband – used to my ravings – looks over with just a hint of fear at my *next big plan*.

'I need to go to B&Q and get the biggest hammer I can find, to throw in the coffin!'

Thankfully, my husband is an understanding but also a logical sort of man. 'OK, but if you throw a hefty old hammer in the coffin, it may go through it and it's going to be hard to explain to your family.'

He has a point! *Rats!* I have to rethink. I still want something that represents a hammer, but it needs to be light.

Then I have another brainwave. 'In that case I'll get a mallet!' A similar shape to a hammer but made from wood and much lighter.

My next problem is how to get the mallet into the coffin. I am not completely heartless toward my dad's family, and because none of them know what he was really like, I don't want to offend them. Therefore, I have to work out how to hide the hammer.

'Plus, I need to get a cushion that I can stuff the hammer into in order to hide it and then throw that in too.'

My husband's lovely, already big brown eyes become even bigger! *Here she goes again!*

On the day of the funeral, I say a prayer – forgiving Dad but also saying a relieved goodbye. I place the hammer within the pillow and take it to the graveside. My husband and siblings know what I am doing. They have been full of grace and have not questioned it; I think they understand. As they lower the coffin into the grave, I throw in the pillow.

Later my dearest auntie comes up to me alongside her daughter, my lovely cousin. 'What was the pillow for, dear?' she asks innocently.

I am not quite sure how to answer and thankfully my wise cousin comes to the rescue. 'Perhaps some things are better left unknown, Mum,' she smiles.

Yes, some things are better left unknown to those that didn't know, but to the knowing they can announce freedom and restoration. No more being smacked by the force of a hammer into submission. No more destruction and violence, psychological warfare and decimation. From now on, the prospects of freedom, space, peace, joy, laughter, hope, redemption and healing are free to enter my life.

# CHAPTER SEVEN

# My Testimony

*Still with unhurrying chase,*
*And unperturbed pace,*
*Deliberate speed, majestic instancy,*
*Came on the following Feet,*
*And a Voice above their beat –*
*'Naught shelters thee, who wilt not shelter Me.'*

Francis Thompson
*Excerpt from* The Hound of Heaven

## Hunted or wooed

I think that if you become a Christian in later life (as opposed to early childhood) then the Lord has to either hunt you or woo you depending on your character. If you respond best to love, he'll woo you; but sadly, if you're a bit hardened, He may need to hunt you. I'm afraid I was so stubborn – and also possibly so wounded – that He had to hunt me. (An abused dog is far more likely to snap at even a loving master, much less want to follow him!)

When the Lord eventually 'hunted' me down aged eighteen, I wasn't much of a catch. In fact, I wasn't much of an anything. All the things that I have written about in this book (and more besides) had had their effect on me. On the surface I looked OK and many friends have said that they had no idea of how I was really feeling. But by the time I was eighteen, I was deeply troubled and broken. In fact, I was suicidal.

The result of being brought up in an abusive home was that I had constant feelings of low self-esteem, inadequacy, fear, confusion, anxiety, powerlessness, despair, injustice, fear of life, fear of being killed, being trapped, guilt, shame, anger, mistrust, feeling exploited, a victim and of no worth.

Life meant battle.

I was also a master at hiding: hiding feelings, hiding sadness, hiding who I really felt I was. I wore a typical clown's mask, laughing and smiling to the outside world, whilst crying underneath. It wasn't that I wanted to mislead people or be secretive; it was simply the way I had been brought up to be. Secrets and (the even more powerful) denial were just a way of life; I didn't know what, let alone who, I really was.

My one source of hope and light in my life had been my beloved grandma. She was actually my dad's mum but bore little resemblance to him in character. She was a strong Cockney lady; she'd had a hard life, growing up in poverty and having to live through the War, yet she was one of the most positive people I've ever met. She was warm, kind and generous, and everybody loved her. She had a wonderful sense of fun and a joy that was contagious.

At weekends and in the holidays, I'd beg my mum to let me stay with her and my gentle grandpa at their bungalow. It was one of my safe places. Everything was ordered and calm. I don't think my grandparents ever knew the horror that went on at home 'behind the closed doors', because I can't think that they would have stood for it. Also, my dad never showed his temper in front of them.

My grandma was amazingly intuitive with me. She could read me like a book and was the only adult that actually understood me. Unlike my mum, whom I had to force to hug me even as a child, Grandma was keen on hugs and playing.

She loved telling stories and making up games and would also occasionally give me compliments, the only person in my life to do so. One day when I was about six, I had been upset because my brother and sister had been teasing me about having freckles. We were on our own, picking plums from her tree at the bottom of the garden. She'd obviously heard them teasing me and yet without referring to them or even looking at me, she said as if in passing, 'My Aunt Mary used to say that freckles were a sign of beauty.' I paused, mid plum. *Well, if that's true,* my little thought process ran, *then I have freckles, so can I be beautiful?* It was subtle and clever but has stayed in my memory ever since, one compliment on top of so many put-downs. She was my lifeline and I loved her so deeply that I worshipped her.

When I was fourteen, suddenly and dramatically whilst we were away on holiday my beloved grandma died. My gentle grandpa had passed away only a few months earlier and I really believed she couldn't face life without him. My dad had got the phone call and in his true, sensitive style he broke the hideous news with two terse words: 'Grandma's dead!'

I was devastated. I went out to be on my own, my body and mind in complete shock. I just could not comprehend a life without her. Then something very strange happened. A feeling, or rather a sense of 'knowledge', came over me that I'd never had before or have had again. Although my grandma had never been regularly to church as far as I knew or even professed a Christian faith, I had an overwhelming sense that she was in heaven.

I didn't even know if there was a God and so certainly didn't believe in heaven, and yet strangely I knew – just *knew* – that she was at *complete peace* there. For me that knowledge was the most real thing that I'd ever had or have ever felt.

But that 'knowledge' raised two questions. If heaven was real, then there must be a God, and if there was a God, why did He take the only person I ever felt properly loved by? I immediately became angry. Then that anger turned to despair. My grandma was my 'god' – I had worshipped her and couldn't live without her – and so began my descent into depression and suicide.

I was still at school and about to take my exams when it happened. Despite having done well in my mocks, I failed all but one of the final exams. I didn't know anything about depression (it wasn't really known in those days that teenagers could get it); I just knew that I didn't want to live.

After a year or two of the symptoms increasing, I eventually read a magazine article about depression and realised that I had it. I told my mum and she offered to get me help by seeing either a doctor or a priest. However, I knew that I was broken-hearted and that neither of them could heal me. My dad, for his part, just said, 'How dare you be depressed. I gave you life! You should be grateful!'

Although I didn't want to hurt the people I loved – my mum, sister, brother and best friends – by committing suicide, eventually the pain got too unbearable and I could no longer put it off even for them. I was eighteen. I thought of the different ways in which I could do it: slit my wrists or with pills?

One day I drove to the house of my lovely friend Glenn, out in the countryside. I thought to myself, 'This is it. I'm going to kill myself on the way there.' That way my loved ones wouldn't have to see me until they had laid me out at the hospital (rather than find me themselves after an overdose or slitting my wrists). I could even picture the wall that I was going to drive into.

Ironically, on that day, for no particular reason, I took a different route and there were no walls to be seen, only trees. 'What about a tree?' I thought to myself – *or did something whisper that to me?* No, a tree wouldn't do! It had to be a wall to ensure that I would smash into it properly and die. However, God had other ideas and there were only trees on that journey and no walls. I lived another day.

Back when I was ten, some new neighbours had moved in next door. We thought that they were mad, fanatical Jesus freaks and I'm ashamed to say we regularly laughed at them, albeit in a fairly gentle way. However, these lovely Christians had been praying for me and my family ever since. I used to regularly 'Granny-sit' their elderly mother when they were away, and one day, because I knew that Jill (the neighbour) had had depression, I decided in my desperation to blurt it out to her.

'I think I'm depressed.'

Without missing a beat, Jill looked at me straight in the eyes and said very powerfully, *'You need Jesus!'*

With that I was off, literally, running out of her house like a rabbit down a hole. 'YOU'RE NOT GOING TO GET ME!' I kept shouting out loud, partly to Jill and partly to God, repeating it over and over as I ran down the road to my house.

I thought she was in some strange sort of cult and there was no way I was getting sucked into that! For the next couple of weeks, though, I pondered. Although we had never been regularly to church, my mum had a very quiet, private faith and it had been around me at school so I knew something about God, although I didn't understand Jesus or the crucifixion stuff at all.

I kept weighing up giving my life to God. In fact, I remember thinking to myself, 'I'm so desperate, what on earth have I got to lose, even if I give Him my life?' I even felt sorry for God if He got me as it didn't seem much of a catch for Him.

I knew that if I did give Him my life, I would mean it. To the best of my ability, I wouldn't take it back. I would obviously still have freedom of choice in all things (God doesn't require us to be a robot or a doormat).

But if I were to enter into a relationship with Him, I knew it would mean willingly submitting to Him out of love. I knew that it would mean His will and not mine had to be done for the rest of my life.

It was a huge ask and it seemed as though He was asking me to jump over from one side of the Grand Canyon to the other, without a net or a parachute or even a guarantee that I would make it. I was absolutely desperate though. It was this, or suicide and nighty-night for ever. Hell might exist or it might not, but to be honest, I was so suicidal that even hell seemed like a relief. *I had absolutely nothing to lose.*

I prayed one night beside my bed, 'I have nothing to offer you, God. I'm all poured out. The only thing that I do have is my life and you can have that, but it's broken and useless.'

I'd love to say that right there in my bedroom at that moment there were angels and clanging cymbals in joyful celebration, but sadly, no, there was nothing. After I'd prayed this though, I had that sense of the Grand Canyon chasm again. It was still terrifyingly deep but this time I realised that what had looked as though it would require an enormous leap over actually only required a tiny step – about an inch wide – and I had made it.

The next morning something *had* changed. As I walked out into the countryside where I lived, it was as though it had been hit with a colour-bomb! Even the normal green of the grass and the blue of the sky, everything had amazingly vibrant colours. I think that I had got so used to my three-year-long depression that even though I loved colour, I hadn't noticed how grey and dull the world had visually appeared to me. This was something new, something beautiful and something that spoke of *hope* for the first time ever in my life.

I was so blessed to become a Christian when and where I did. I started to attend a local, very vibrant and busy Anglican church. It had that wonderful mixture of solid theological teaching, an openness to the Spirit, a relevance to real life and, for me most importantly, a belief in God's healing power. God also blessed me with three wonderful women – Jill, Ruth and Joy – who were experienced in praying for emotional healing and who recognised how badly I needed it. I was desperately thirsty for God and His teaching, and especially His love.

I began what I can only describe as a wonderful 'honeymoon' period with God. For the next nine months, He showered me with a sense of His love for me, through prayer and music, church, other Christians and His word. In His mercy, He began those first steps toward repairing all of that damage that had been done to me, and has continued ever since. He is faithful.

## Prayer of commitment

Perhaps after reading my testimony you feel drawn to either giving or re-surrendering your life to God? If you do, then it might be wise to think and pray it over as I did, in order to count the cost, as God tends to take us at our word if we make promises!

If you still feel sure, then this is the sort of prayer you could use:

*Dear Lord,*

*Thank you that you love me just as I am. I give my life and my heart to you now and I choose to live for you.*

*I know that I have made mistakes in my life, so please would you forgive me and cleanse me through Jesus your Son's sacrifice. Thank you, Lord.*

*Please would you come now and fill me with your presence, your Holy Spirit, to guide and to comfort me. Thank you that you have good plans for my life. Please lead me now into the future and help me to always stay faithful to you.*

*In Jesus' name. Amen.*

# PART TWO

# Manual of Hope

# CHAPTER EIGHT

# Freedom

*Therefore my dear ... sisters, stand firm. Let nothing move you.*

*1 Corinthians 15:58 (TNIV)*

## The roots of abuse

Perhaps after reading my story of living with an abusive man you have recognised that you have had the same experience? The second half of this book aims to help you to start to recover from that abuse.

Why does abuse happen?

In Genesis we see that sin enters the world and, as a consequence, Eve is told:

> *'Your desire will be for your husband and he will <u>rule</u> over you.'*
>
> *Genesis 3:16 (emphasis added)*

This word 'rule' or *radah* in the Hebrew literally means, 'to have *dominion* over, to rule over, to reign, to prevail against, to tread, to trample, to chastise'[23].

As Christians we believe that Jesus came to break the curse and consequences of sin.[24] Therefore, no longer is the husband to 'rule over' his wife. Paul exhorts:

---

[23] *Strong's Concordance.*
[24] See Romans 5:12-21; Galatians 3:13.

> *Husbands, love your wives as Christ loved the church and gave himself up for her.*
>
> *Ephesians 5:25*

Rather than dominating his wife, a husband is to now love his wife as much as he loves himself and she in return can then respect him.[25]

As Christians the 'gold standard' of a marriage is one of mutual love, respect, honour and care.

## Recovery from the dominator

At the beginning of this book we learnt that a perpetrator of domestic abuse is a 'type' of person. This type of person's main aim is to dominate and control their chosen 'victim's' life.

They will do this through a variety of methods including psychological and physical intimidation. These methods are chosen to contribute to brainwashing their victim into believing certain things about the perpetrator and themself. It is vitally important to recognise that *these are all based on lies!*

It is important to the abuser that the victim believes that she has:

- no self-worth;
- no choices in life;
- no support network;
- no independence;
- no abilities;
- no rights;
- no hope or way of escape;
- no strength.

It is also important to him that she believes that *the abuse is all her own fault* and therefore *her* own responsibility, that it is because she is so worthless that she deserves to be treated badly. It is important to the perpetrator that the victim believes that he:

- *is not* following a considered campaign of abuse;
- has no control over his abusive actions;
- loves her so much and that this is why he behaves this way;

---

[25] See Ephesians 5:33.

- *is not responsible for any of his actions or behaviour.*

In this second part of this book we are going to try to counter the lies of the perpetrators with the ultimate weapon: God's truth. We are going to look at:

- how God feels about abuse;
- how He feels about us as women;
- how He created women to be;
- what scripture says about women;
- which scriptures have been misquoted to support abuse;
- how healing from abuse is possible;
- how to pray for healing.

## The truth will set you free

We saw in Genesis how the Lord predicted that males would 'rule' or 'dominate' over females. Dominion means to 'rule over', 'to tower over' and 'to control people arrogantly'.

Do you recognise your dominator? How does he do this? Ultimately, in order to gain control over you, the dominating man has to make you believe that you have no power, no control, no choice and no worth in or of anything. *Wow!* That's quite a feat.

He is a master manipulator. Some will go to any length, even including death (yours, your family's, your friend's or even his own sometimes) to ensure that you believe what he wants you too. He deals in the kingdom of lies and darkness.

- His major lie is that you are powerless – powerless in *every* area of your life.
- His second lie is that you have no control of *any* area of your life or even of yourself.
- His third lie is that you are worthless.

Can you see how the Father of Lies, the enemy, is behind all of this?[26] Yes, our fight is not against flesh and blood, though it sure does feel like it most of the time.[27] But our main fight is against a principality and a

---

[26] See Job 8:44.
[27] See Ephesians 6:12.

power that wants to steal, kill and destroy you and possibly those you love.[28]

The good news is that, as believers, we have not only the most powerful source in and above all creation fighting our corner, but we also know the *ultimate* truth. I can't put this strongly enough into words, and even as I write this, my prayer is that every single one of you reading these words would believe these ultimate truths about your state of being in Christ.

The truths that will set you free are:

- YOU ARE WORTHY (John 3:16).
- YOU ARE POWERFUL (Romans 8:11).
- YOU DO HAVE CONTROL (Romans 8:9).
- YOU DO HAVE CHOICES (Deuteronomy 30:19).

If you are willing, please repeat these words aloud to yourself:

- I AM POWERFUL!
- I DO HAVE CONTROL!
- I CAN MAKE CHOICES!
- I AM WORTHY!

Start to allow these truths to sink into your thinking.

## Be brave

Now, wait a minute, I hear you cry, when my lover is slamming my head against a brick wall, I don't have control over him! When my lover has just raped me, I'm not powerful. When he's told me for the fiftieth time today that I look fat and called me an ugly wh\*\*\*, I don't feel worthy.

It is true that at any point your abuser is in an act of abuse against you, he has some form of dominion over you. Nonetheless, your abuser can't maintain his dominating abuse over you *incessantly;* even he has to eat, sleep or go out occasionally. In those times when your abuser is absent, pray and start to change your mindset; start to try to gain some of your power and worth back again.

For example, do you remember in the news the 2002 Ohio case, in the USA, of the four young girls who had been kidnapped by a man

---

[28] See Job 10:10.

named Castro and kept locked in a house? Some of them for twelve years! They were subject to constant rape, beatings, starvation, childbirth, spontaneous abortions, chains, darkness, imprisonment, psychological abuse and mind control.

Well, these amazing and brave girls owned their power, control and worthiness! Even after all those years of abuse, when their abuser had gone out to work and mistakenly left the door unlocked, they managed to call for help.

*They were rescued.* Imagine if after all those long years of disgusting obscenity, they had believed their abuser's lies?

'We're powerless! We have no voice; we can't call for help!'

'We've no control! We have no strength; how will we escape?'

'We have no choice but to remain in this hell-hole until we die!'

'We don't deserve to live in the fresh air and in safety, with loving family and friends around us!'

Those girls were inspirational in the way that, after all that abuse, they owned their power – and you can do it too! They refused to have a victim mentality and they refused to settle for despair. They took their power and used it for their own sanity and survival's sake, and you can do it too.

## Some keys

Although you have been masterly manipulated, in fact brainwashed, into a prison of believing lies, *you* hold the keys to your own prison. If you are a Christian, your keys consist of believing and acting in the ultimately powerful Kingdom of God's rule and reign.

Your keys are in God's truth, and what He says about you.

What does He say?

- He says that as a woman you were made in His image (Genesis 1:27). He is a mighty God, therefore you are a mighty, strong and powerful woman (Genesis 2:18).
- He says that the same power that raised Christ from the dead is alive in you (Romans 8:11).
- He says that the prayers of a righteous woman are powerful and effective (James 5:16).
- He says that you are an overcomer because the one that is within you is greater than the one who is in the world (1 John 4:4).

- He says that you can do all things through Christ who gives you strength (Philippians 4:13).
- He says that you are so important to Him and so worthy that He was willing to give you His most precious thing, His Son, in order that you might be created, saved and able to spend eternity with Him (John 3:16).
- He says that He is your rock, your fortress and your deliverer (Psalm 18:2,3).
- He says that your worth is more precious than gold, silver and rubies (Proverbs 31:10; Job 23:10).
- He says that His Spirit 'does not make us timid, but gives us power, love and a sound mind' (Timothy 1:7).
- He says that He delights over you – more than that, that He tumbles and wheels over you – in His delight at your beauty (Zephaniah 3:17).
- He says that when He made you, you were very good in His sight (Genesis 1:31).
- He says that He will never leave nor forsake you (Hebrews 13:5).
- He says that though the mountains be removed and the seas dry up, His love for you will never be shaken (Isaiah 54:10).
- He says that you will sleep in peace because He will be your safety (Psalm 4:8).
- He says that you are His crown (Isaiah 62:3).
- He says, 'Do not be afraid, you will not suffer shame' (Isaiah 54:4).
- He says, 'Do not fear disgrace; you will not be humiliated' (Isaiah 54:5).
- He says that He is for women, not against them. He honours them so much that He entrusted the *whole* of humanity's salvation to one woman, Mary (Luke 1:28).
- He says that He will have 'everlasting kindness' and 'compassion' toward you. (Isaiah 54:8).
- He says, 'The Lord will call you back as if you were a wife deserted and distressed in spirit – a wife who married young only to be rejected' (Isaiah 54:6).
- He says that He is mighty to save you (Zephaniah 3:13).
- He says that He is 'an ever-present help in times of trouble' (Psalm 46:1).

This is how God sees you and this is how precious you are as a person in your own right and definitely before Him. God believes that you deserve a good life, that you deserve freedom and light, safety and peace, love and respect. Do you believe that too?

# CHAPTER NINE

# Tender to my Daughters

*Sing, O Daughter of Zion, shout aloud O Israel! Be glad and rejoice with all your heart, O Daughter of Jerusalem! The Lord has taken away your punishment, he has turned back your enemy. The Lord, the King of Israel is with you, never again will you fear any harm.*

*Zephaniah 3:14,15*

How does God feel about us as His daughters? How does He think we should be treated and what does He think and do about the abuse we have suffered?

For some reason, I seem to have many very close friends who have been victims of physical, psychological or sexual abuse. I have listened to these always beautiful (outwardly and inwardly), kind, funny, warm, lovely women as they occasionally mention memories about their abuse.

They speak quietly and often underemphasise the horrors that some of them received from the hands of family members or 'friends'. Many of them are Christians and as I have listened to their brave recollections and yet know their undoubting faith, I have grown angry.

Obviously, I am angry at their abusers who have knowingly ripped the innocence and joy from their lives. However, due to my own abuse I know that these abusers, however vile in their sins, are still human and therefore imperfect by definition.

However, one day as I considered it, I became incensed with anger toward God. How could a loving Father who doesn't just promote love but *is* Love do this to my beautiful friends? How could He just stand back and watch as these poor women had to take all of that horror on their own?

I started to shout. In fact, I started to rant at God. *How dare He allow that?!* 'Where were you in all of that pain and all of that loneliness? How dare you, God?! How dare you do that to my beautiful friends?'

The answer came swiftly and not without a strong sense of knee-trembling awe – not fear, I assure you, but pure, awesome *awe*. He was dramatically authoritative and sincere but without any sense of domination. There was a real sense of a lion roaring (like Aslan in *The Lion, The Witch and the Wardrobe*) and yet a breathtakingly holy, steely, strong quietness in his reply.

He said, *'I am tender to my daughters!'*

He spoke with such passion. Yet also with a gentle kindness and sadness toward me, that I could possibly doubt His love for us as women, His precious daughters.

Even now as I write this, and every time I describe this or think of it, I start to cry. I cry because I can still feel His pain as He said it. His pain was because His love for us as women is so vast and so powerful.

He so wants us to be safe and not to be hurt. In fact, it was hurting Him that I didn't even recognise His love or, more accurately, *couldn't* even see it. How dare I, and how could I as one of these beloved daughters question His integrity or His love for each of us?

I think about that now when I am talking to women who have been subjected to vile abuse from humans. Although I reel at their suffering and what they have had to bear, I also remember that it is *not God* who is the cause of their suffering. It is not He who has come to rob, steal and kill; it is not He who metes out unbearable punishments.[29]

Quite the opposite; it is He, Christ, who has provided a way out of that suffering, a way of healing of the atrocities that have been done. It is He who has taken all the pain, all the horror and obscenity, upon Himself because of His great love for us. It is true, He has not prevented the pain (I will explain why later) *but He has cured the pain.* It is He that is tender to His daughters, if only we will let Him be.

## The psalm of the abused

Before I started this book, I went on a week's retreat. One day as I was praying in tongues, I felt the Lord was giving me the interpretation of them and I wrote it down. A dear friend of mine, the beautiful Natalie,

---

[29] See Job 10:10.

remarked that it was like a psalm. I wanted to include it in this book, because if you are a woman who has suffered domestic abuse, I want you to know how your loving, heavenly Father feels about it and about your abuser. Here it is:

### Too Long

Too long!
Too long they have been stolen from me,
My daughters from all the generations.
You will crush Satan beneath your heel.
You are mine, you were bought with a price.
Say to the captives, the daughters,
Pronounce freedom,
Freedom to those that suffer,
Freedom to those that weep.

They are not their own, they were bought at a price;
Too long you have suffered, too long!
I have heard their cry.
I _am_ a God of justice;
I will break the chains that bind them,
They will call to me and I will answer them.

Too long! Too long!
'There is no one to save us.
No Father in heaven.
No one to release us.'

Their pain is searing,
Their tongues stick to the roof of their mouths.
There is no one to rescue them,
So they believe.

No longer will they call you Deserted
Or Desolate.

'Papa!'

I am disgusted with those men.

*They are a disgrace*
*In their arrogance and pride.*
*They have no sense of justice or truth.*
*I stand against them;*
*I turn my face from them.*
*Too long! Too long!*
*They have succeeded*
*But their time is coming;*
*The time is very soon*
*When they will be no more*
*And my women will lie down in safety.*

*The battle is long and costly.*
*Battle on!*
*Victory is always at hand,*
*The task will succeed,*
*Love never fails.*
*Bring liberty to the captives, Alison;*
*For such a time as this you were born.*
*I will show you who the captives are.*
*Don't be afraid!*

I want to reassure you, if you have cried out to God at any time, He has heard you and He is answering you. He loves you passionately and wants you to be free and happy. Keep listening for Him.

## Love is...

*The Lord will call you back as if you were a wife deserted and distressed in spirit – a wife who married young, only to be rejected.*

*Isaiah 54:6*

'Love is...' There used to be a sweet series of cartoons about a loving husband and wife and their lives together. So, for example, one caption read, 'Love is... being able to say you're sorry,' with a cartoon of the man explaining whilst the woman was crying. They were a comment on what 'love is' really like and how a couple should ideally share their love.

As we have seen, an abuser wants to brainwash you into believing his lies about certain things in order to continue to promote his abuse and power over you. He will even go so far as to try to change your perceptions of what 'love is' and what makes for a healthy relationship.

Now, if you are willing to, I want you to do an exercise to bring out into the light the lies of the enemy who is speaking through your abuser. Many of you who will know the well-loved reading from Corinthians 1:13 in the Bible. It is often read out at weddings and is a staple for describing the characteristics of love.

Your abuser will undoubtedly tell you at times that he loves you; that his love is powerful and strong for you, that it is unlike any other man's love. He will try to persuade you that his words and actions are those of pure love, that no one loves you as well as he can (when he's in the mood for it).

Now, if you are willing, I'd like you to do a little experiment. Please get hold of a Bible and read those verses in 1 Corinthians 13:4-7, out loud: 'Love is patient, love is kind...' and so on.

Now take some time to consider *all* of your abuser's behaviour – not just the times when he is being lovely or 'charming the birds from the trees' but also the times when he is verbally abusing you, or threatening you, playing psychological games with you or beating you up.

Does it fit in with the Bible's description of love?

I would suggest that an abuser's version of the 1 Corinthians verses about love would really read like this, as this is how he treats you. (If you are willing, try slowly reading this aloud and see the difference between the two.)

> *'Love' is impatient, 'love' is unkind. It does envy, it does boast, it is proud. It dishonours others, it is self-seeking, it is easily angered, it keeps records of wrongs. 'Love' delights in evil and hates the truth. It always harms, always distrusts, always despairs, always gives up. 'Love' always fails.*

Can you see how one minute although he might be declaring his enduring love for you, at other times his behaviours and words are not love but the opposite? They are hate. Their roots are evil, as evil is the opposite to love. Let this truth start to sink in and undo the lies about his 'true love'.

## Don't give your abuser yet more power

*...you, who through faith are shielded by God's power.*

*1 Peter 1:5*

Although abuse is hideous, I have learnt the hard way through many years of counselling and prayer that it pays us (the sufferers) to maintain a certain level-headedness of opinion about the power and influence of our abusers.

During one of my counselling sessions, I had put my father's 'temper tantrums' down to him being 'a psycho'. The counsellor said that this was extremely unlikely as psychotic people are very rare. (But then, she had never lived with him, I reasoned in my head!)

However, one point that was made to me in counselling was that to a child of an abuser, that person seems huge and beyond human. They take on only shades of dark and no goodness can be found in them. This is then not helpful as it gives the abuser an inordinate amount of power.

This is also not a Christian perspective. We know that *all* humans are made in the image of God and are therefore sacred, as is God. They also, therefore, no matter how damaged or influenced by evil, have to contain some amount of good or love. (For example, even Hitler loved animals, poetry and painting! Please don't misunderstand me; *I am not* defending Hitler or his atrocities to humanity.)

Try to remember that although your abuser may seem completely evil and powerful, he is just flesh and blood, the same as you or me. Don't give him more power by elevating his status into pure evil. Our fight is not against flesh and blood but principalities and powers.[30]

Please don't mishear me; I'm not saying that abusers aren't dangerous or life-threatening. A sad fact is that they are. But what I am saying is to *remember that you are equal to him in power and status in Christ.* Don't make him into a monster that can't be beaten.

*Because he can.*

## To honour is to be truthful

*Honour your parents.*

*Exodus 20:12*

---

[30] See Ephesians 6:12

My father was a complex mixture of darkness and light. During many years of healing prayer and counselling, I have found this truth becomes helpful both in honouring someone and in forgiving them.

When I became a Christian I was keen to keep the fifth commandment ('Honour your father and mother'), if only so that 'all may go well' with me, if I was honest. Yet how could I admit what my dad had done, seek help or even tell others, and still honour him? Surely to be truthful already implicated him.

I believe that honouring your parents (or your abuser) is not complying or agreeing with anything that they have done wrong. In fact, it is admitting the opposite, the disagreeable truth (as appropriate), and yet in balance it is also admitting what was good in them.

I have written here of some of the things that were the dark side of my father but as I have gone deeper into healing and therefore deeper into forgiveness, I have been able to admit all that was good in him. I owe a lot of my physical characteristics and interests to him and his genes. My father gave me: Celtic colouring of dark hair and green-blue eyes; a bumpy nose; a dodgy hip; a second toe bigger than my first but also a good pair of legs! He also gave me a love of: speed; adventure; risk-taking; toffees; strength; passion; music; cars; food; swimming; Guinness; and James Bond films!

The tricky part of an abuser is that he will have a degree of good in him, albeit that it sometimes gets used to evil and devastating ends. I am not saying that the good in any way negates all the evil that he does, and in some ways his manipulation of the good within makes that evil all the more devastating. What I am saying is that for your sake of healing and wholeness, it is OK to admit what was good, without losing sight of what was evil. If you make him completely evil in your mind, it will give him too much power, so that he can forever haunt you or keep you in fear. He wasn't a huge, all-powerful monster but was in fact just a human being, like you, a mixture of good and bad. Seeing him from this perspective is the truth and is more balanced. It therefore gives you the power to reduce him down to size, whilst taking his power of intimidation away. (It also makes it easier to forgive him, which benefits you.)

## Why does God allow domestic abuse?

> *What if God, although choosing to show his wrath and make his power known, bore with great patience the objects of his wrath – prepared for destruction? What if he did this to make the riches of his glory known to the objects of his mercy, whom he prepared in advance for glory – even us.*
>
> Romans 9:22,23

At the beginning of this chapter I briefly summarised why abuse exists at all.[31] However, if we see from a Christian perspective that abuse is the result of sin and yet we still believe that God is all powerful, He adores us and is 'tender to his daughters', why does He *not stop abuse?*

The theological debate regarding love and evil is huge! But it is still important to consider it in this book, especially as it is a question that I had to grapple with on becoming a Christian, considering my painful childhood.

I mentioned in chapter 9 that actually it pains God to see us suffer as His daughters. The Lord is not heartless and cruel, nor is He impotent, and it is not His delight to see us abused and unloved.

In fact, the Lord loves us so much that has had to make the huge sacrifice of just standing by – in one sense – whilst horrific atrocities happen to His most beautiful jewels of creation. As any good parent has witnessed, it is great suffering to see your children suffering and yet be unable to interject. But God is all-powerful – surely, as a loving Father, He would interject and physically stop the abuse?

Yet what if He did? What if He stopped every single evil act of every single person here on earth? What would that look like for you and me, and what effect would that have on our lives? To think of it somehow reminds us of heaven. However, we know from experience that He won't always stop evil; so why not?

## To allow free will is to love

To understand this, we have to look at how John describes God. He says in 1 John 4:16, 'God is love.' What is one of the most important characteristics of love? It is the opposite of dominion; it is freedom.

---

[31] We will look at this in greater depth in chapters 10 and 11.

If God were to take away human free will, He wouldn't be 'Love'. *To allow free will is to love.* If humans weren't given any choices, then that would mean that they were no longer free but subject to His control and, as we know, control isn't true love. Pure Love is to be free to choose, even if it runs the risk of people choosing evil over good, which we frequently do.

Our Lord is not powerless. Quite the opposite; Jesus as fully man (so that He can understand our pain) but also as fully God (so that He has the power to deal with *all* of humanity's pain and sin for all of time) has taken the most powerful course of action in all eternity: the cross.

His sacrifice of complete suffering and surrender has rendered all acts of the enemy null and void. The enemy has no power over us as believers, and even the acts that he tempts people to do (or sometimes makes them do) are rendered useless through the healing that Jesus provides.

## For the love of us

The cross is a barbaric and yet beautiful testimony. It of course does speak of suffering, unimaginable pain and isolation; it is the ultimate martyrdom. It is the God-man taking all of human suffering for all of time upon His own self.

But why? Why does Jesus willingly put Himself in that position? He does so because the Lord *loves us.* He loves us with an overwhelming, endless, inseparable kind of love. The kind of love that leads Him to give up everything for His beloved: us. Have you ever loved that way? I have, when I would willingly have given up everything for the one that I loved. It is powerful and it is beautiful.

Jesus defeats death and comes back to life. He wins that eternal life for His beloved so that we can be forever together. He offers us life in all its fullness whilst we are here on earth. He offers us freedom from pain whether that is emotional, physical or spiritual.

He offers us a good life with a good plan and a hope for a beloved eternity. His sacrifice has meant that we are able to access His healing power. This healing can be physical, psychological, emotional or spiritual, but it is real; I am a witness to that.

## Prayer

*Heavenly Father God,*

*Thank you that you love and care for me, that I am not on my own and that you are always with me. Thank you that your word says that in you I am strong, powerful and of sound mind. Thank you that I have choices and that I am worthy of being loved and respected.*

*Please give me your wisdom about how to handle my abuser's lies and his behaviour. Please show me the way forward into the life that you want me to have.*

*In Jesus' precious name.*

*Amen.*

# CHAPTER TEN

# The Bible as a Weapon

*For the word of God is living and active. Sharper than any double-edged sword, it penetrates even to dividing soul and spirit, joints and marrow; it judges the thoughts and attitudes of the heart.*

*Hebrews 4:12*

In my research about Christian women who have been abused by Christian males, it struck me how many of the men used the Bible as a defence and sometimes even a reason for their abuse. Therefore, it felt imperative in this type of book to include a chapter on God's word; how perpetrators can twist it, texts that are often misused or abused, the reality of what the Bible actually says about women, and how I believe God views us as His beloved daughters.

## Shame equals silence

The shame of abuse is huge. For the Christian being abused by another Christian, especially their husband, it is even larger. Although the abuse is not her fault *at all*, somehow, the fact that someone in her own family is behaving in such an un-Christian-like manner makes it nearly impossible to bring the abuse into the light. We are called to be the 'salt' and the 'light' of the world, so to admit that your husband is abusive shames not only your own witness but his too, and, you may even feel, Christ's.

If your husband then also happens to be the pastor, you lose not only your and his reputation, but your church, your calling and often your home and your income. The costs of abuse are huge; no wonder so many women struggle to admit the truth and would rather continue in a life of abuse than face all of those penalties.

As a note of interest, look at these statistics. Although they are fairly out-of-date now, sadly, from experience, I know that in some UK churches today they still stand. In 1985, a survey of conservative USA Protestant Clergy showed that 21% of them believed that no amount of abuse could justify a wife leaving her husband. A shocking 26% believed that a wife should submit to her husband come what may and that God would either give her 'a way out' or the 'forbearance' to withstand any amount of abuse![32]

Compare that to the statistics in my first chapter, of the number of women murdered by their 'lovers'. Does the Holy God really want the female part of His creation to be decimated in this way? Where is the love and justice of Christ in a Church that condones that?

Therefore, if your abuser is a Christian and is using the Bible as a tool with which to condone his abuse, it is imperative to look at what it says about males and females and how we relate to each other, and our 'roles'.

## Power to harm or to heal

Committed Christians believe that the Bible is *the word* of God. Generally, we know that words spoken or written by people in their own right have a lot of power (to harm or to heal[33]).

However, God's word has the ultimate power in all of heaven and for all of eternity. It has dominion not just over the outer physical world but also over the inner emotional, psychological and, of course, spiritual world that we inhabit. For example, we know that all of creation was made by the spoken word[34] and that John refers to Jesus Himself as 'the Word'[35].

The power that is contained in the word of God can therefore become a type of tool, and as any tool it can be used for good or harm depending on the intention of the person using it. For example, a hammer can build a beautiful house or cause a fatal head injury; a fire can make a nice barbeque or burn your house down.

---

[32] Taken from *Why Does He Do That;* Lundy Bancroft; Berkley Books, Penguin Group (New York, 2002); page 322.

[33] See Proverbs 12:18.

[34] Genesis 1:3

[35] John 1:1

The bad news is that in the 'wrong hands' this tool can be used for harm; especially within the hands of an abuser, where it has the power to break down, destroy and take dominion over his victim.

However, the good news is that for the abused woman, the word of God is an absolute and literal God-send. In the 'right hands' it has the power to comfort, heal, change, build, encourage and transform her life for the better.

Perpetrators often use the Bible as a tool to aid their abuse in these ways:

- the misquoting of biblical texts;
- taking the word of God out of its context;
- using scripture to create an atmosphere or culture (whether that be in the home or the church) where women are seen as inferior to men in the eyes of God.

## Using your Christian theology against you

As we know, perpetrators are devious. They are able to use not just scripture but also your own Christian theology against you to aid their abuse.

The Bible teaches that as believers we are meant to follow Christ's example of behaviour and language in treating one another with respect, forgiveness and love. This principle is especially important within marriage and the family context.[36]

These are all good Christian qualities. However, God is wise enough to recognise that these qualities can make us vulnerable to those that would take advantage of them. Therefore, He protects these qualities by putting biblical 'guidelines' or 'principles' around them.

Perpetrators will often demand that you show these qualities toward them (and will wrap them up in texts). *But,* they will conveniently forget to remind you of the surrounding guidelines! Without these guidelines the perpetrators know that their victims are vulnerable, and it allows them to continue their control and domination, seemingly backed up by the Bible.

For example, he may state, 'It doesn't matter that I've given you a black eye and a cut lip. Jesus said that you have to forgive me *no matter what* and *take me back!*' Now, your abuser knows that as a Christian

---

[36] See Ephesians 4:1-6; 5:25; 1 Timothy 3:12

you believe that Jesus taught, 'Forgive seventy times seven,'[37] and that, Paul taught, 'Bear with each other and forgive whatever grievances you have against each other.'[38]

But what your abuser doesn't mention are the guidelines that both Jesus and Paul gave around the subject of forgiveness. For example, four verses before that 'forgive seventy times seven', Jesus stated, 'If your brother [or husband] sins against you, go and show him his fault, just between the two of you. ... But if he will not listen take one or two others along ... If he refuses to listen even to them ... treat him as you would a pagan or a tax collector.'[39] In other words, approach him as a non-believer!

The principle Jesus teaches here is to always forgive. But the guideline is that you have a right to point it out if someone hurts you (and later with witnesses). And if they won't listen, i.e. they keep hurting you, you have a right to treat them as a non-believer or a 'tax collector'. In that culture tax collectors were not very welcome!

(Caution: please don't think that I am suggesting that you go now and confront your abuser through this; it is merely an example. Please pray for God's wisdom in this. If your abuser is determined to abuse, you could probably take the whole angelic host of heaven to witness to him and he'd still deny it!)

Again, Paul's advice of, '...forgive whatever grievances you have against each other,' is in the context of Paul talking about being in fellowship with others in the Church.[40] He advises to *forgive all sin,* but also he tells *all* the believers to rid themselves of 'anger, rage, malice, slander and filthy language'[41].

Therefore, the guideline would be, if your abuser is using any of those against you then yes, you forgive him. But you don't have to put up with that behaviour and others have permission to 'teach and admonish'[42] him. (Though they need to do so very wisely.)

Jesus and Paul taught that *it's imperative that you continually live in forgiveness,* but that it is also imperative to hold people to account for

---

[37] Matthew 18:22
[38] Colossians 3:13
[39] Matthew 18:15-18
[40] Colossians 3:12
[41] Colossians 3:8
[42] Colossians 3:16

their sin and to react accordingly *if they don't change their ways.* You have Jesus' permission to forgive but also to protect yourself; here is the proof.

## Women, be silent!

Another example of an often-misquoted biblical text that is a hammer in the perpetrator's toolbelt is that of insisting that the Bible says that you, as a woman, are to 'be silent'[43]. Whenever he commands it, of course... Wow, that's a powerful one! With one quick swipe and three little words backed up by a biblical reference (out of context), he has managed to take your voice, and silence must reign.

What's in that silenced voice? Your character, ideas, beliefs, vision, identity and, of course, defence. Why would you want to have any of those? Why would God want you to have any of those? Well, *He does!* You are made in His image and He is a communicating God, after all, who delights in giving us our character, ideas, beliefs, vision, identity and defence.

In fact, as we shall see later, the very adjective that God uses to describe womankind when He creates her relates to her ability to communicate. We will put this 'silence' quote in its proper biblical context later, but for now be aware that as Bancroft states in his excellent book about male abusers:

> *A woman with no voice is the dream girl of many abusive men.*[44]

Please decide now not to be that 'dream' girl! Please decide to use your voice to speak out, whether that is to show all of your beautiful character, hopes and dreams, or to tell of his abuse when the time is right, to get help and healing.

## The dangers of headship

> *Submit to one another out of reverence for Christ. Wives, submit to your husbands as to the Lord. For the husband is the head of the wife as Christ is the head of the church, his body, of which he is the Saviour. Now as the church submits*

---

[43] 1 Timothy 2:12.
[44] See reading list on page 146.

*to Christ so also wives should submit to their husbands in everything. Husbands love your wives, just as Christ loved the church and gave himself up for her to make her holy, cleansing her by the washing with water through the word, and to present her to himself as a radiant church, without stain or wrinkle or any other blemish, but holy and blameless. In the same way, husbands ought to love their wives as their own bodies. He who loves his wife, loves himself. After all, no one ever hated his own body but he feeds and cares for it, just as Christ does the church – for we are members of his body.*

*Ephesians 5:21-30*

Although at present it is a hotly debated topic in theology, many Christians believe that the Bible teaches that a man or a husband is the 'head' of the woman or his wife.[45] This type of 'headship', as they understand it, implies hierarchy and that the woman is inferior to the man – not necessarily in worth, but in the sense of leadership of the family unit, the church and areas of society. Therefore, the man has the God-given right to have the 'last say' when leading and the woman has to be submissive to his decisions.

There is much debate over these verses, and in the following sections on Ephesians 5 and 1 Corinthians 11, we will look carefully at the Greek words Paul uses that are translated as 'submit' and 'head'.

If this is the belief system held by you and your husband (especially if this is backed up by your church) then… *please be very careful!*

What better theology could a perpetrator have than that *you must do all that he demands and at his slightest whim?*

For example (and, sadly, these are true examples):

- If your husband decides that you're literally to, 'Lick the floor clean, woman!' and he is the head of the household and you *have* to submit to him, then the licking has to commence!
- If he wants to have sex despite the fact that you have only given birth seven days before and your stitches are still in, then you will have to be submissive and have undoubtedly painful, unpleasant, if not dangerous, sex. After all, that is his God-given right! Or is it?

---

[45] See 1 Corinthians 11:3.

Whether this idea of headship as we understand it is correct or not, it still has to be seen in context. The context that Paul in Ephesians puts it in is that of *loving* households. He first states (in verse 21), 'Submit to one another'.[46]

Also, if this idea of a hierarchal headship is correct then the husband has some duties too within this household! How much should a husband love his wife? 'Husbands love your wives *as Christ loves the Church*' (verse 25, emphasis added) and 'husbands ought to love their wives as their own bodies' (verse 28). Therefore, how should he treat her? 'He feeds and cares for [her]' (verse 29). How much does Christ love the Church? Well, He sacrificed himself for her (see verse 25), not the other way around!

Your abuser might pick scriptures to back up his abuse but ultimately I don't believe that there is any scripture that promotes his treating you with mistreatment or disrespect. In fact, if you, your husband or your church believes in this kind of 'headship' and insists that you 'submit' to him, then he has an absolute duty to treat you *at all times* with total love, respect, support, care, protection and cherishing.

After all, if his calling is to always take the lead in your household then he has to always lead as Christ did, who 'made himself nothing by taking the very nature of a servant'[47].

## Let's play consequences

As we have seen in Genesis, abuse enters the world through sin. Another misnomer that has sometimes been apparent in Church culture is that it was Eve (womankind) who tempted the poor, innocent man Adam to sin. Apparently, he was way up at the back of the garden and out of earshot, nowhere near Eve when she was tempted...

Although it does state that it is Eve who is deceived by Satan, where is Adam at the time? Read Genesis 3:6:

> *She also gave some to her husband, <u>who was with her,</u> and he ate it.*
>
> *(emphasis added)*

---

[46] It may help you to read this Ephesians text in Eugene Peterson's version of the Bible called *The Message*. He describes it in a way that seems more sympathetic to what Paul seemed to be aiming at.

[47] Philemon 2:7

Eve is deceived but Adam is not; he knows that what he is doing is disobedience against God, as Paul states in 1 Timothy 2:14.

Now we come to what is possibly the most telling part of the Bible that explains the abuse of male against female. Sin has consequences; ultimately it leads to death but even before that, things are going to get rough, to say the least. Part of the woman's consequence of sinning is that, 'Your desire will be for your husband and he will rule *[radah]* over you.'[48] As we've seen, *radah* literally means, '*to have dominion over, to rule over, to reign, to prevail against, to tread, to trample, to chastise*'[49].

The man's ruling power doesn't seem to have an inclination towards kindness and mercy. Instead it seems to be inclined towards negativity and, worse still, a trampling, treading over, chastising kind of power – *if that is what he chooses* (and it is worth adding here that many men don't.)

Ouch, that's a harsh power to live under! But amazingly, women are still going to want to be with men. In fact, the woman will have a 'desire' (*teshuqah* in the Hebrew, a 'pull' or a 'turning' toward the male[50]). This word can also mean 'a longing' or a 'stretching out' toward him.[51] Women will continue to love men even if they're mistreated by them!

On a practical level this also explains why so many of us can keep on loving and putting our hope into men who clearly don't respect us or treat us equally. Our 'pull' toward him can be our weakness; it can make us more vulnerable, which then makes it easier for the man to dominate.

If we look at the majority of races and cultures worldwide, we see a fact that backs up the prediction of Genesis. It is obvious in the world that males tend to dominate females and there is a worldwide culture of patriarchy, regardless of a nation's creeds or socio-economics.

But is that how the Lord wants it to continue? Or is bringing in God's kingdom rule and reign through Christ about mutual love, equality and respect between the sexes?

---

[48] Genesis 3:16
[49] *Strong's Concordance.*
[50] Guinness, Michelle; *Woman the Full Story;* Zondervan (Grand Rapids, 2003), page 47.
[51] *Strong's Concordance.*

# CHAPTER ELEVEN

# An Encouraging Bible Study

*...reflecting God's nature. He created them male and female.*

*Genesis 1:27 (MSG)*

Let's now look at scripture to see what God actually says about womankind. I am the first to admit that despite having a degree in theology, I am not an expert in the fields of Ancient Hebrew or Greek! However, due to my own abusive background, I have looked in detail at the scriptures to try to better understand many of the difficult passages concerning male and female relationships within Christ.

We will look at both the Old and New Testaments on this subject, although unfortunately only brief points can be made on each passage as space dictates. However, do please research this and ask God to speak to you about how He sees womanhood and how men and women are to relate to each other.[52]

## A 'good' idea!

> *Then God said, "Let us make man in our image, in our likeness ..." So God created man in his own image, in the image of God he created him; male and female he created them.*
>
> *Genesis 1:26,27 (emphasis added)*
>
> *God saw all that He had made, and it was very good.*
>
> *Genesis 1:31*

---

[52] There is a book list at the back of the book, which you might find helpful.

Let's look again at how male and female relationships were from the beginning. In Genesis 1:26-27 the Godhead (Father, Son and Spirit) decide to make humanity in their own image, so humans are created, 'male and female'. Therefore women are made in God's image just as much as men.

God makes Adam from the dust, the earth, which his name actually refers to. God then makes Eve, the woman (whose name means 'life-giver') from Adam.[53]

Now, even here at the very beginning of Genesis, language interpretations of the biblical Ancient Hebrew start to cause problems for us as ladies.

## The help?

> *The Lord God said, "It is not good for the man to be alone. I will make a <u>helper</u> suitable for him."*
>
> Genesis 2:18 (emphasis added)

In preparation for this book, I began by researching the Hebrew meaning of God's description that He pronounces over us as women in the above verse from Genesis. In our modern-day English bibles, the woman is weakly called the 'helper'. Worse still, this translation describes her *only* in terms of being the man's help.

In the past, there has not been proper emphasis on the fact that the male's life was not 'good' without her, that her creation was an absolutely necessary act. Life in Eden pre-fall was meant to be *very* good if not perfect for the man, and yet it was not good without her existence. Moreover, it has not been widely recognised that in order for the man to be helped, the Lord needed to create a human with some skills, knowledge or strengths that he didn't already have. (What would be the point of a carbon copy?)

## God's description of womankind

I believe (as many theologians do) that there has been a tragic disservice in the interpretation into English of the Hebrew words that God uses in Genesis 2:18 to describe womankind. Our poorly interpreted modern-day translations speak of the 'helper' or even 'suitable' 'help

---

[53] *http://answeringgenesis.org/human-body/from-dust-to-dust*

meet'[54]. But in the Ancient Hebrew she is called the *Ezer Kenegdo;* 'helper' is an extremely watered-down version of what these actual words mean.

Why is this translation a problem for women (and incidentally men) today? In the English language and Western culture, we particularly find that the term 'the help' has connotations of hierarchy, with the 'help' always being of a lower status. It also implies a sense of weakness or inferiority about that person. For example, a maid, cleaner or even servant is often referred to as 'the help' within households. Sadly, this type of interpretation can then also empower males (and particularly abusers) who believe that womankind was created to be a type of servant or, even worse, slave to the male.

## Wonder Woman!

In fact (and I can't state this strongly enough), God's name for womankind, the Hebrew word *Ezer,* has a far more powerful meaning than just to help. It has two roots to it and these refer to both 'power' and 'strength'.[55]

Other meanings attached to it are 'to rescue or save, to protect, defend, surround and cherish'.[56] *Ezer* appears approximately twenty times in the Bible and each time it is only applied to the Lord God Himself, bar one time when, amazingly, *God* uses the same name to describe womankind before He creates her.[57]

Now, why would the Lord God, when He decides to create womankind, give them the same name and description as Himself? Is it because He is trying to point out that there is going to be something unique about 'woman'? That her 'role' is meant to be one of a position of strength and power in order to rescue, protect and cherish those around her?

In the Bible, we see that God is called on by the name *Ezer* when men are in trouble or hardship, especially if losing in times of battle. Then they call out to be helped and rescued by their 'helper', *Ezer,* God. If this

---

[54] KJV

[55] *God's Word to Women; http://godswordtowomen.org/ezerkenegdo.htm* (2013), pages 1-2.

[56] Ibid.

[57] Ibid.

name then denotes power, strength, rescuing, saving, defending and surrounding, no wonder it was used when facing defeat![58]

This does not mean that women are as powerful as God or that He sends in the women to sort the poor little boys out if they're in difficulty. Obviously not! We know that man is part of God's wonderful creation. We know that he is also made in the image of his strong and protective God and is called to be such (in Christ). Plus, we know that a woman's role is not to be placed above a man's (or we'd be back to square one, with domination).

However, could it be that male and female are to put their differing strengths and abilities into working together in unity (just like the Godhead)? Could it be that for this reason it wasn't good for the man to be alone? God didn't supply his need with a weak, unstable, inferior appendage. What kind of help would that be? Instead, God in His perfection gave him a powerful and strong *Ezer,* 'she' that is made in His image.

## The daughters of Eve

It is interesting to think that perhaps God also calls womankind 'Eve', 'the life-giver', because the majority of her daughters will also bring life into the world through bearing children. They are the ones who will protect, defend, surround and cherish those vulnerable lives in their womb and once delivered. In fact, one woman in particular, Mary, will bring the eternal Author and Perfecter of Life into the world. It is she who will give birth to the ultimate *Ezer* – Rescuer and Saviour – in whose image she is made.

## Does she remind you of anyone?

In practical terms, do these descriptions not sound like some of the women you know? Not only can they be powerful and strong, but the majority are lovingly intent on protecting and defending their relatives and friends, especially if any of them are in need or at risk. (Ask a mother, a loving wife or a friend what length she'll go to in order to protect her loved ones and she'll probably liken herself to a lioness or a tiger on the rampage!)

---

[58] See, for example, 2 Chronicles 14:11.

Women have not only the ability, but also a strong desire, to cherish and surround their loved ones. Godly men too will want to protect and nurture but in a way that is different to women. It is interesting to note that Jesus likens Himself not to a father but to a mother hen wanting to gather and hide her chicks when He speaks of His loving, protective feelings toward Jerusalem.[59]

This is what Almighty God says of women: that they are both powerful and strong. It does not back up the weaker maidservant theory; quite the opposite in fact.

## The two sides of a coin

The other word that God uses to describe how He has made womankind is *Kenegdo,* which is attached to the word *Ezer.* In most English translations of this in the Bible, we get the description of womankind being 'suitable' for the man, in order to match his needs, with connotations of her being 'acceptable' to him and 'right for purpose' (like a well-fitted suit or a comfy pair of slippers!)

However, again this Hebrew word has a more powerful meaning and connotation. It comes from the word *neged* which means 'counterpart', 'opposite', 'in sight of' or 'corresponding to' another.[60]

Therefore, Eve is Adam's opposite half. When God brings her into view for the first time (literally 'in his sight'), he realises that she matches him and corresponds to him unlike anything else in all of creation.[61] They are like the two sides of a coin, on opposite sides to each other, looking different but of equal value.

## You talk too much!

God pronounces over Adam, 'It is *not good* for the man to be alone.'[62] Up until this point Adam is a solitary creation, a one of a kind. Even the animals are not the *Ezer Kenegdo* that God has in mind for him. Therefore God, in His loving mercy and wisdom, creates for Adam a 'good' *neged*. Besides meaning an opposite or counterpart, this word can also mean 'to communicate' or 'to tell'. What will cure man's loneliness

---

[59] Matthew 23:37
[60] Ibid.
[61] Genesis 2:23
[62] Genesis 2:18 (emphasis added)

and isolation? Undoubtedly, some company. But what sort of company: an unspeaking animal or someone made like him and in God's image, i.e. a verbal communicator?

Therefore, God creates Eve for Adam as a literal correspondent. She is the only one who can relate to him in the same way, and only she has the ability to communicate with him, human to human. This is ultimately to be for his good, despite the fact that if may get 'for better or for worse' later on!

## Females are 'as much' as males

Within the centre of God's word for womankind, the *Ezer Kenegdo,* is a little but very interesting Hebrew word that is inserted before *neged.* This word is the *ke* or 'k' sound.[63] It is sorely overlooked in interpretations and in fact we don't even have it in the English translations, but this tiny word in the Hebrew can mean, 'like, as, according to, as many, as much, as often, equal'[64].

In other words, the female has the same value as the male. She is made his 'opposite', but also God makes her 'as' he is: 'as much', 'as often'. The Oxford English Dictionary notes that the word 'as' means, 'used in comparison to indicate extent or degree'. The Hebrew states that that degree or extent is the same for female as it is for male. Compared to him, she has the same extent or degree of ability or worth: 'as much, as often, as many'.

In other words, she is the other side of that coin spoken of earlier. Whichever side that coin falls on, it is of equal worth and has equal 'spending power'. Could it be that here, right at the beginning of time in Genesis, God is stating that Eve corresponds to Adam, an opposite but an equal?[65]

## A worthier translation

To summarise then, a worthier translation of womanhood in Genesis 2:18 tells of God creating another 'good' human being who is opposite yet corresponding to Adam. She is to be strong and powerful, and has

---

[63] Ibid.

[64] *Strong's Concordance*

[65] *God's Word to Women; http://godswordtowomen.org/ezerkenegdo.htm* (2013), pages 1-2.

the ability to save, protect, defend, surround and cherish those she loves. She is 'as' Adam, 'as much' and 'as often' 'equal' to him and created to be in 'communication' with him.

God in His mercy and love has gone to all of this trouble to prevent Adam from being alone, possibly even lonely, which is not good for him. All of these interpretations of the Hebrew are far more powerful than of the English translation of just being a 'suitable helper' for the male.

Please meditate on these truths contained in God's word if your abuser uses scripture incorrectly to preach 'at' you. He may say that as a woman you were made as an add-on to creation, a lesser being, almost an afterthought of God, created just to be a weaker 'helpmate' and therefore subservient to a man, and particularly him.

However, that is not what our lovely Lord has pronounced over us as women. Although we know that our 'fight is not against flesh and blood'[66], the enemy will use your abuser and his lies to try to hold you captive and weak. Please don't accept it! It is not God's truth.

## Women in the Old Testament

Bearing in mind that the Old Testament is written at a patriarchal time, it is amazing how many stories about women and their achievements make the grade. Even here we see that God is pro women and wants them to be treated fairly.

For example, look at Zelophehad's daughters in Numbers 27. Due to the death of their parents and because they had no male relatives, their inheritance would have been lost under the old patriarchy laws. In order to survive they call on Moses for equality of land rights and Moses then enquires of the Lord. What does God say to him?

> *What Zelophehad's daughters are saying <u>is right</u>. You must certainly give them property as an inheritance.*
>
> *Numbers 27:7 (emphasis added)*

God cares about His daughters, their rights and their survival.

## Women as leaders

If women were created to take a lesser hierarchal role in leading and decision-making in society then some testimonies of the Old Testament

---

[66] Ephesians 6:12

don't make sense. In fact, it is interesting that God puts the very survival of the Israelite nation into the hands of women at several points in history. Here are some examples:

Moses, who will eventually lead *the whole nation to freedom,* has at least six strong and powerful *ezers* (women) quite literally saving, rescuing, protecting, defending, surrounding and cherishing him throughout his life.

First, we see the brave protection of the midwives, Shiphrah and Puah, *saving all the Israelite boys* from annihilation by being disobedient to Pharaoh.[67] The third woman is his *risk-taking* mother who *saves him* by hiding him for his first three months. She then makes the ultimate, heart-breaking sacrifice of possibly losing him and even killing him by putting him in a basket into a river.[68]

Fourth, we see his sister, most likely Miriam the prophetess (who will later *lead the nation* with him to freedom)[69] *watching over him* and *bravely* facing Pharaoh's daughter with a clever plan *to save him.*[70] Pharaoh's daughter herself is rescuer and *cherisher* number five, adopting him as her own son and bringing him up as a prince.

Finally, strong defender and life-saver number six will be his wife Zipporah. In a very strange part of this story, God is about to kill Moses.[71] However Zipporah, through circumcising her son (and therefore being obedient to God), *intervenes and so saves Moses' life,* 'so the Lord let him alone'[72].

Despite this being a patriarchal society, we see women such as Deborah, prophetess, judge and expert in battle strategy, *leading the whole Israelite nation for forty years of peace after defeating the Canaanite king.*[73] Within the time that Deborah leads the nation, another powerful woman, Jael, *defeats Sisera, the commander of the enemy army,* with her own bare hands by driving a tent peg through his head![74]

---

[67] Exodus 1:15-17
[68] Exodus 2:3
[69] Micah 6:4
[70] Exodus 2:4-10
[71] Exodus 4:24
[72] Exodus 4:26 (NIV)
[73] Judges 4 and 5
[74] Judges 4:22

Queen Esther (a trafficked bride, no less) negotiates successfully again for her *whole nation's survival*.[75] Huldah, the prophetess, is the only one able to give King Josiah God's instructions concerning *the survival of Judah*.[76]

Is all of this the work of weak 'helper' women or maidservants aiding only the men? Or are they strong and powerful *ezers*, designed and directed by God; rescuing, saving, cherishing, defending and protecting, when people, nations or even the whole of humanity are in trouble?

## The lie

Has your abuser ever told you that the Bible states that you are a weak, lesser add-on of a human being, an unstable, stupid, emotional slave or servant to him or to males in general; whose only role in life is to be a child-bearer, a cleaner, a cook, a domestic being? Well, he's *lying!* The Bible states no such thing.

## The New Testament

God's word states that He regards women with the utmost of respect and love, and then Jesus comes to earth to prove it. Read it for yourself in the Gospel of Luke and see how Jesus treats the women that surround Him. It is always with respect, love, compassion, encouragement and worth.

Look at who the Lord God Almighty gives the first ever gospel preach and job of evangelism to. Who is it? Could it be the *neged*, the communicators?

> When they [the women] came back from the tomb, they told all these things to the Eleven and to all the others.[77]

Luke even names these women:

> It was Mary Magdalene, Joanna, Mary the mother of James.[78]

Wow! The most important preach and witness of all time, and God gives it willingly it to His women. Sadly, the next verse shows that even

---

[75] Esther 8
[76] 2 Kings 22:18
[77] Luke 24:9
[78] Luke 24:10

114

Jesus' disciples (apart from Peter) didn't respect the women's amazing testimony.

> *But they did not believe the women, because their words seemed like nonsense.*
>
> Luke 24:9-11

## Paul's letters

It is vital to remember that the Bible has to always be seen in its own context. Paul's letters were at a specific time in history and to specific people groups, within a certain culture, and therefore should be read that way.

This does not mean that they are not applicable now, far from it. Paul was a brilliant theologian, and I believe God inspired him to write truths that would stand up for us until the end of time. However, to not see scripture in context is extremely dangerous.

I will briefly cover the main areas of Paul's writings that perpetrators of abuse use against women.[79]

### 1 TIMOTHY 2:11-15

> *A woman should learn in quietness and full submission. I do not permit a woman to teach or to have authority over a man; she must be silent. For Adam was formed first, then Eve. And Adam was not the one deceived; it was the woman who was deceived and became a sinner. But women will be saved through child-bearing: if they continue in faith, love and holiness with propriety.*

With one fell swoop Paul here appears to tell women that they can learn but must be silent; they cannot teach men or have leadership authority over them. They must be submissive and can only be 'saved' by child-bearing.

Let's put this letter into context. Paul is writing some advice to Timothy – a young, inexperienced leader – about his congregation, to try to contain some of the problems the church is experiencing. This church had been recently established in a city called Ephesus. As the church grew, it started to gain converts to Christianity from a wild and debauched

---

[79] There's a book list at the back if you want to look into this in detail.

female-dominated cult called the cult of Artemis. Artemis was a god of fertility, served by thousands of young flamboyant female attendants and male (unsurprisingly) *eunuch* priests.[80] In fact, it placed females in hierarchy *above* males as priests and teachers, and it was also anti-marriage and anti-family. Drugs and sex were used to 'help' the cultic followers to prophesy, and these prophecies would have been shouted out willy-nilly, so to speak.

Paul, in this letter, is advising Timothy about how to deal with these new converts who are assuming that this new type of 'temple' (or church) that they have joined will be run in a similar way to their own. Therefore, he instructs against shouting out prophecies without any respect or order. He wants to uphold marriage and family values rather than cultic fornication and adultery. In short, he is stating that God's kingdom values are more worthwhile than this cult's beliefs.

In this passage Paul reaffirms equality of male to female (2:13), marriage (4:3), respectful teaching and learning (2:11) and having children (15).[81] Verse 12 is often translated as 'to have authority over' but it can also be translated that a woman should not 'domineer over' a man.[82]

So the emphasis is that women are not to dominate men (just as men are not to dominate women)[83]. This especially applies whilst teaching them. Paul, like Jesus, doesn't want the Church brought into disrepute by being outside of the cultural norm, unless that norm is evil, for example, child sacrifice, incest, creating eunuchs, fornication etc.

If the above is not the correct interpretation, then there is an inconsistency in the argument of those who believe that women cannot teach men. For example, if Paul is against females teaching males then why does he commend Timothy's *female* relations for *teaching* him well?[84] Why does he allow Priscilla with Aquila to *teach* Apollos, a learned male Jew, in Ephesus?[85] Why does he send a woman, Phoebe,

---

[80] France, R. T.; *Women in the Church's Ministry;* Paternoster Press (Carlisle, UK, 1995), page 58.

[81] Ibid., page 60.

[82] Ward; *Growing Women Leaders;* page 29.

[83] For example, 'Submit to each other.' (Ephesians 5:21)

[84] Anderson (ed.); *Men, Women and Authority;* page 122; referring to 2 Timothy 1:5; 3:15.

[85] Acts 18:26

with his letter, which is a *teaching duty*?[86] And why does he pronounce Junia (who many theologians throughout the centuries believed was a woman) an outstanding *apostle*?[87] Why does he not denounce their teaching also?

It is also worth noting that Paul says, *I* do not allow in the following instructions. At no point does he say, *God* does not ever allow... Surely, if he were making a point for *all* churches for *all* of time, he would have stated that. However, if this is a specific situation for a specific context then he is more likely to make it personal advice.

## 1 CORINTHIANS 14:33-35

> *For God is not a God of disorder but of peace. As in all the congregations of the saints, women should remain silent in the churches. They are not allowed to speak, but must be in submission, as the law says. If they want to enquire about something they should ask their own husbands at home; for it is disgraceful for a woman to speak in the church.*

Many theologians agree that Paul – like Jesus – was unusual in that he believed that women should learn about scripture. Up until the time of Jesus, the Jewish patriarchal systems only allowed males to learn. Then Jesus rocked the boat by allowing Mary to sit with other males at His feet,[88] which was a traditional learning stance for a tutor's pupils.[89]

Paul stated, however, that when females were taught, they needed to learn in silence and submission,[90] which is similar to our learning style for adults today. Male novices in that culture were also expected to learn in silence. The word 'shameful' or 'disgraceful' can also mean 'culturally inappropriate'.[91] Therefore, if men were to learn in silence, then so were the women.

Paul believed in orderly worship and so he didn't want women who were learning, and therefore curious, interrupting the worship with their

---

[86] Romans 16:1
[87] Romans 16:7
[88] Luke 10:39
[89] Ward; *Growing Women Leaders;* page 35.
[90] Anderson (ed.); *Men, Women and Authority;* page 122.
[91] Beck and Blomberg; *Two Views on Women in Ministry;* page 50.

queries. Instead, they were to direct their questions to their husbands at home in order to learn, which seems reasonable.[92]

If Paul was stating that *all* women, for *all* time and in *all* churches, should remain silent, why did he use the words 'when women prophesy'[93] (which presumably refers to women in the church speaking out) in the same letter? This would seem to imply that he is contradicting himself in his own letter...

1 CORINTHIANS 11:3-12

> *Now I want you to realise that the head of every man is Christ, and the head of the woman is man, and the head of Christ is God. Every man who prays or prophesies with his head covered dishonours his head. And every woman who prays or prophesies with her head uncovered dishonours her head: it is just as though her head was shaved. If a woman does not cover her head she should have her hair cut off; and if it is a disgrace for a woman to have her hair cut or shaved off she should cover her head. A man ought not to cover his head since he is the image and glory of God; but the woman is the glory of man. For man did not come from woman, but woman came from man; neither was man created for woman but woman for man. For this reason and because of the angels, the woman ought to have a sign of authority on her head.*
>
> *In the Lord, however, woman is not independent of man, nor is man independent of woman. For as woman came from man, so also man is born of woman. But everything comes from God.*

This is a very unusual and complicated passage to understand in our culture, and again theologians argue over the correct interpretation. Many believe that it is about doing what was culturally appropriate for that time and place. (For example, only prostitutes would leave their heads uncovered in that society and men were not allowed to wear head coverings whilst worshipping.) Whilst others believe that it backs up the 'headship' theory of males being in hierarchy over females.

---

[92] 1 Corinthians 14:35
[93] 1 Corinthians 11:5

118

For 'head', Paul here uses the Greek word *kephale*, which can mean either the part of a human's physical anatomy or *the source* of something. In the same way in English we talk about 'the head of a river', meaning the source of that river. However, in English we also use the word 'head' to mean 'boss' (e.g. the head of a company), but *kephale* does not have this meaning.

In verse 3 Paul could be stating that the *original* source for man's life was Christ and the *original* source for woman was Adam and the *source* for Christ was God. This seems to make sense when later[94] Paul argues that now, *in the Lord,* men and women cannot be independent of each other; that just as *a* man was the original source for *a* woman, ever since then *men* have only been born via *women.* Paul here seems to be referring to the circular shape of life rather than a triangular hierarchical shape.

If so, we see this idea repeated again in Colossians where Paul states about Christ being the *kephale,* or 'head of the body'.

*He is before all things and in Him all things hold together.*

*Colossians 1:17*

In other words, to put it more graphically, if you are beheaded your source of life is gone and it renders the rest of your body pretty useless! If Paul here also meant *a person's physical head,* this would explain why he goes on to discuss actual head coverings and hair lengths for *both* sexes.

Some state that this passage refers to males being in hierarchy above females, as God is above Christ in hierarchy. These believers think that this hierarchy is linked to 'role subordination' between the Father God and Jesus.[95] However, others hold that this belief, that Father and Son are not equal, is a heresy.

ROMANS 16:1-2

> *I commend to you our sister Phoebe, a servant of the church in Cenchrea. I ask you to receive her in the Lord in a way worthy of the saints and to give her any help she may need from you, for she has been a great help to many people, including me.*

---

[94] verses 11 and 12
[95] Ward; *Growing Women Leaders;* page 41.

Here we see Paul commending the carrier of the letter to the Romans, a lady called Phoebe.[96] Usually the carriers of his letters would have to explain and fill in any details that the churches might need to know. *This was a teaching duty,* and presumably not just to the females of the church.[97]

EPHESIANS 5:21-30

> *Submit to one another out of reverence for Christ. Wives, submit to your husband as to the Lord. For the husband is the head of the wife as Christ is the head of the church, his body, of which he is the Saviour. Now as the church submits to Christ so also wives should submit to their husbands in everything.*

Most of this text was covered in the section entitled 'The dangers of headship'[98]. An additional point worthy of mention is that English translations uses 'submit' as the first word. Submission in English means 'to yield; to obey; to be meek, obedient'[99]. Here, submission appears to deny choice, strength and discussion. The word 'submission' even conveys an image of one person being allowed to dominate another, with the dominated one being forced into obedience. For example, in a game of rough-and-tumble between siblings, an older, stronger brother may fight and then sit on the younger one. What does he then shout? 'Submit!' In other words, 'Give up your rights; I've overthrown you!'

This *language of force* does not seem to comply with Paul's overall ethos throughout the New Testament, where he goes to great lengths to try to create harmony, unity and equality between all of the believers.[100] Why would he then insist that dominance should be found in the family and home and liken it to his beloved Christ and the Church? This would seem at odds with the rest of his arguments.

The Greek word Paul uses that is here translated 'submit' is *hupotasso*. This word means 'to put in order' or 'to get under and lift up'. Therefore, in modern day English a more accurate interpretation

---

[96] Beck and Blomberg; *Two Views on Women in Ministry;* page 197.
[97] Ibid., page 38.
[98] See page 102.
[99] Oxford English Dictionary.
[100] 'There is neither ... male nor female for you are all one in Christ.' (Galatians 3:28).

would be, 'Be a willing support...'[101] Or, as Eugene Peterson puts it in *The Message* (MSG), 'Out of respect for Christ, be courteously reverent to one another.'

In our present context of the English language, can you see how to 'support' or to show 'courteous reverence' is a far more voluntary and reasonable suggestion than to submit? If your husband is loving you and supporting you as much as Christ does the Church, then why on earth would you not want to support him? But only if he is!

## Dig deeper

I have offered you some basic explanations of these verses, but I would urge you to do your own research about God's word and how it relates to women.

## Prayer

> *Dear Lord,*
>
> *Thank you for your life-giving word. Through the power of the Holy Spirit, please would you give me an increasing knowledge of your word and speak to me through it. Thank you that you love me and that you made me to be a woman, strong and with a purpose. Lord, if my abuser ever uses your word against me, please help me to be able to hold on to what I know is the truth.*
>
> *In Jesus' name.*
>
> *Amen.*

---

[101] *God's Word to Women;* 'Articles', submission by Sandra Clements.

# CHAPTER TWELVE

# Healing

*By his wounds we are healed.*

*Isaiah 53:5*

As I stated at the beginning of this book, over the last thirty years of my being a Christian, the Lord has been healing me very gently (and very slowly) of all of the hurts that I have received through abuse.

In one way this process has been easy, because I was desperate to become happier and more whole when I became a Christian. That was my goal and I recognised that only in Christianity can this be achieved, after I had looked at many other world religions. However, in other ways it has also been hard at times and it has taken a great deal of perseverance. I have had to set a definite course of being willing to face the pain of certain events again. And I have had to trust that God is able to heal me, no matter how impossible it seems.

I can honestly say that He has never let me down or failed me; He has always come through. The healing may not have always happened in the way I wanted or according to my timetable, but it has always been perfect.

## How do you know what to pray about or what needs healing?

How does God speak to you about what He needs to heal in you? His voice is everywhere if only we will listen. It's particularly in prayer, through other believers, sermons, prophecy, words of knowledge, talks and books. But I've also been prompted by the Spirit whilst watching films, listening to music, going for a walk or listening to friends (and sometimes enemies). In fact, God is God and He can use anything He likes to speak to us (just as He once used a donkey!)[102] His voice will always be gentle and loving; anything that seems dominating or controlling is not Him. Sometimes He speaks firmly, but nonetheless very gently in that 'still small voice'[103].

What follows are some examples of the many ways in which God has healed me over the last thirty years. I have put these in for two reasons:

- Hopefully my testimony will encourage you that if you persevere and want to be healed, then the Lord is not only able, but is willing and waiting for you to be healed and made whole. I believe He wants this so that you may have a happy life and not be haunted or affected forever after by the effects of your abuse.[104]

- So that if you are new to this type of healing you can see how it works. (Later, I will give a step-by-step guide as to how to pray for emotional healing.) However, if you are seeking healing and are not experienced and not in a church environment that encourages it, then do be careful; this type of prayer can make you very vulnerable and you need to feel that you can completely trust your prayer partners. This is especially true due to your abuse, as any dominating or inexperienced prayer can do more harm than good. Therefore, I suggest that you only pray with Christians who are experienced in this type of prayer and with whom you feel safe and comfortable spiritually. If there is nobody like that in your church, then do get in touch with recommended healing ministries instead.[105]

## Breakfast at Tiffany's

> *The Lord will surely comfort Zion, and will look with compassion on all her ruins; he will make her deserts like Eden, her wastelands like the garden of the Lord.*
>
> *Isaiah 51: 3*

It was a rainy Sunday afternoon, in the days of only four channels on the TV and Sunday closing. My sister and I settled down to watch an old film. Quite often it would be an old Hollywood spectacular – Astaire and

---

[102] See Numbers 22:21-33
[103] 1 Kings 19:12
[104] See John 10:10
[105] There is a list of healing ministries at the back of this book

123

Ginger with all the glamorous dresses and dances that we loved. Today, however, it was an old 60's film, but nonetheless a classic, called *Breakfast at Tiffany's.*

Due to my upbringing of control and abuse, I had swung the pendulum in the opposite direction and become a rebel with a well-defined sense of 'freedom' and wildness (as opposed to being trapped and having to conform to another's complete will). This meant that I loved not being tied down to anyone or anything. I had no sense of commitment and I was happy with that. I saw myself as untameable, a rebel with my own cause. In all areas of my life, if I liked it (and it didn't hurt anyone) I did it. If I didn't like it, I didn't have to do it, listen to it, be with it or put up with it (and that included people). I was a free bird! Although this attitude was somewhat normal as a non-Christian, it produced problems for me as a Christian when I found out that I was called to be a 'living sacrifice'[106]. How could I submit to authority, be committed to a cause or a person, let alone my faith, as such a free bird? How could patience, mercy and forgiveness grow without the earthy soil of sacrifice and being yoked to Christ? If I loved my life, I had to lose it. God challenged me.

In *Breakfast at Tiffany's,* the main character, Holly Go-Lightly, has similar values to those I had. In her bid to escape poverty, boredom and mourning she has invented a new self of glamour, status and 'freedom'. Her freedom involves non-commitment (she takes several lovers to 'pay' for her lifestyle) and non-ownership (she never settles anywhere, has little furniture in her flat and won't even name her cat). In reality she is a call girl with little hope, and life has a nasty habit of crashing in on her. As she watches her world crumble about her, all her plans of 'escape' dissolve and she is left with an unwanted but faithful lover. In the final dramatic scene, she argues with this admirer who states that he loves her and that she 'belongs to him'. She refuses his love and says in response that she doesn't want to be 'put into a cage'. Her admirer is about to propose but reality bites and he speaks the truth to her, that basically she thinks that she's wild and free but, really, she's already in a cage and it's one of her own making, because wherever she runs she'll just keep running into herself.

As I watched this, it was as though the actor was speaking directly to me, as God's Spirit convicted me: 'This is you, this is what you do; it looks like freedom but it's actually a trap because only doing things God's

---

[106] Romans 12:1

way will bring you freedom, however upside-down it seems. Your 'freedom' of non-commitment and no self-control stops you from knowing the joy of being steady and secure, of being measured and even, quiet and strong, of even having a life partner.'

I arranged to get help. I called some ladies in the church who I knew would pray for my healing, and I met them and prayed. The Lord was faithful and healed me. All because of a classic film on a rainy day! God is omnipotent!

## The school run healing

I described previously how, as a small child, I had been sworn at and smacked about the face on the way to my first school by my dad. Forty-two years later I was praying with some friends for yet more emotional healing from my dad's treatment of me.

I had prayed about this incident before as actually I had had to renounce a self-curse, an inner vow I had made about not having my own children if that is how they got treated. However, I felt that I was to pray about this again, and this time I saw it differently in my memory. I was once again in the cloakroom of my first school, sitting on the metal piping, hiding amongst the coats and shoe bags all hung on the pegs with the pretty, colourful pictures of animals and letters above them. I was looking at the floor and crying, but then something lovely happened. There was a sense of someone who was gentle, beautiful and friendly, playing a game of 'peek-a-boo' with me, peering through the shoe bags and coats. He was laughing and smiling. It was Jesus, keeping me company and playing, letting me know that it was all going to be alright. I wasn't alone and I wasn't rejected; He was with me and I was safe.

## Healing for standing up to Dad

*I will repay you for the years the locusts have eaten...*

*Joel 2:25*

I was praying through some emotional healing when my lovely prayer partner Liz had a picture. She saw a little girl aged about five who was in an Arctic wasteland; there was nothing but ice and snow around her. The girl was pulling a sledge behind her with the rope attached about her waist, and on the sledge was an incredibly heavy load but she couldn't tell what the load was. I knew immediately that the girl was me and I knew that the load was my family, my mother and my siblings. I was trying to fight my way across a very vast and barren land in my own strength, yet pulling them along with me. I saw it as *my* job. I saw myself as responsible for my family's complete safety and survival.

We prayed about the fact that no one had asked me to do this job; I had taken it upon myself and I had to repent of that, as it was never God's will for me. The job was too huge and I was too small for all that responsibility and the sheer weight of it. As I prayed repentance and asked for forgiveness, we prayed that I would be cut free from this burden.

As Liz prayed, I saw in my mind's eye a taut tightrope around my middle break; then suddenly a weight was lifted from me. It was interesting because I had always walked with a stoop, slightly bent over – for many reasons – but as we prayed I could feel my body and back literally straighten up and I felt a physical sense of lightness over me. In my mind's eye, as this rope broke I suddenly became free to stand up straight and to run. As I ran away from the sled, I saw that Jesus was standing in the distance straight in front of me. I couldn't see His face very well, but I could tell it was Him. He was bearded and was wearing fur clothes, and was facing me, completely joyous and radiant. As I saw Him and ran toward Him, He flung His arms open wide. I jumped into them and He flung me round, so happy were we that I was at last free from that massive burden. He is good!

## The victim

Another time was a little less glamorous. I was having (secular) counselling and my therapist mentioned a little word to me in response to something I had talked about. The little word was 'victim'!

I was horrified and replied in defence.

'I'm not a victim! I'm a survivor!' I exclaimed, without trying to sound like a *Destiny's Child* song.

I went home, my feathers distinctly ruffled. I was upset and hurt, but I prayed and pondered. As I sat still before the Lord, I was able to measure objectively what she had said and her reasoning. After a while of soul-searching, I came to the conclusion that she was right! Although I was strong and brave at certain times, I also often went into self-pitying mode, letting myself believe, 'I have no power in this situation,' or, 'I can't do anything about this, I'm trapped,' or even the self-pitying

'Nobody likes me; I'm going into the garden to eat worms.' (Not literally, of course!)

Once I had accepted this truth about myself, that I did at times think of myself as a victim, I was able to weigh it up. Do I want to be a victim? Is that in any way attractive to me or to others? I knew the answer immediately: *definitely no!* So I asked the Lord for forgiveness and healing, and allowed to Him to speak to me, minister to me and free me from a pattern of being that was in itself a trap.

## Fear

> For God did not give us a spirit of timidity, but a spirit of power, of love and of self-discipline.
>
> *2 Timothy 1:7*

God is amazingly gracious. When I first became a Christian, I had the absolute privilege of being invited to pray with three gorgeous Christian ladies for spiritual and psychological healing.[107]

'What would you like prayer for?' they asked.

'Fear,' I replied.

'Of what?'

'*Everything...*'

'You can't be frightened of *everything!*' they exclaimed.

Yet this was exactly how I felt. All things contained fear in them because my childhood had been either ruled by or subject to constant fear from the womb. My whole being had been keyed into survival mode. Have I done too much or too little? Are they all cross with me? Do I have to walk through this room alone? Are they going to kill me? Are they talking about me? Fear in those early years of being a Christian was a constant area in which I had to have healing prayer.

## The truth shall set you free[108]

Another way God healed me has been by convicting me by His Holy Spirit as I have either heard God's word preached or I have read my Bible. God shines the spotlight, perhaps on attitudes I have or certain behaviours that are not godly, and if I am wise, I listen.

---

[107] Thank you to Gill Rainey, Joy Chipchase and Ruth Gee.
[108] See John 8:32

I don't always agree with God at first; sometimes I argue or disagree, but I always try to keep an open heart, just in case I'm wrong! If it's genuinely the Spirit convicting me, I'm always 100% wrong! Then it's a case of coming in humility before the cross of my lovely, gentle Lord and saying sorry, asking Him to show what the root cause of the problem is; nine times out of ten your behaviour won't be stubborn disobedience but due to the fact that you yourself have been hurt. Then I ask Jesus to forgive me for my part in it, I forgive whoever hurt me (remember, forgiveness is a choice not a feeling) and then I ask Him to cleanse me by His blood and heal and restore me. He always shows up.

## The prodigal's brother

One day I heard the story of the prodigal son. Personally, I didn't identify with the naughty son but with the naughty brother. The prodigal's sins are easy to spot, the brother's are more complex. I had always felt sorry for the brother in this tale; after all, he worked hard. He didn't ask for anything and he was loyal and kind to his father. Did he really deserve the telling off he got?

Well, yes. Why didn't he ask his father for anything? Did he not trust him to give generously? Was he jealous of the relationship between his brother and his father? Why did he judge not only his brother's sins but also his father's attitude toward his other son? God was challenging me: 'Isn't that how you see me? Do you think that I am not happy with you; that I don't long to bless you too with good things?'

## 'Do you trust me to be kind or am I a mean God?'

Another time the Lord spoke to me through the parable of the talents. I was the scared one that buried the little I had in the hope of not getting found out. Why was I scared? Because somewhere deep in my heart I still believed that God was like my earthly father – not to be trusted and mean.

## Deep to deep[109]

Some of my healings from abuse are so deep that it is impossible for me to fully understand or to explain with words what happened. Instead, I describe them as 'deep to deep'; only the Spirit of God can know how

---

[109] See Psalm 42:7

He ministers to my own spirit on that level. These healings are always beautiful though and their effects are always to produce a wholeness and space that only the oppressed can really know about.

One time a couple were praying for me and particularly about all the physical beatings that I had ever received. They started when I was in the womb so obviously there's no way I could remember them. However, as they started to pray, I felt a tremendous weight of misery come upon me. It sunk me, literally to my knees, lower and lower until I crumpled on the floor and all I could do was to cry. As we asked Jesus to minister to me, I could feel the weight lifted from me; I became light and airy, and joy entered my heart in some places for the first time. Deep to deep.

## Merry-go-round healing

At the beginning of this book, I described my childhood life at home as being like a hellish merry-go-round. This image was given to my dear friend Clare who was praying with me once. She described it like this:

'I see a picture of you as a little girl and you are seated on a horse on a merry-go-round. But as you turn around to look at me, I can see that this isn't a fun ride but that you are scared and appalled and in terrible pain. The merry-go-round itself is coloured in red and black and the horses aren't friendly but scary; the whole thing looks horrific and hellish[110]. You can't get off the ride and it won't stop but it just keeps going round and round and up and down in an eternal cycle.'

By this point I was crying because it was such an accurate picture of how it had felt as a child. There was no escape and no way of stopping the horror. I was just relieved that someone was witnessing it. We asked the Lord to heal me and, as He did so, the picture changed. Clare explained:

'Now I see the same merry-go-round but this time it is beautiful. It is painted gorgeous colours and is bright and cheerful. This time you are looking over your shoulder and your face is a picture of pure joy and laughter. You always have a choice as to when to get off or stop it too.'

---

[110] Another friend who had prayed with me felt shocked when the Lord had showed her that my childhood had been like living in hell.

## Walk out your healing

Sometimes the Lord heals us and all that He requires us to do is to be honest about our feelings and open to forgive and receive His blessings. At other times He may require us to be more practical or actually 'walk' our healings out.

For example, due to all of the abuse from my dad and the ridicule about my weight and looks, I suffered from a chronic fear of not being able to enter or walk through a room crowded with people. I think I felt that I was going to be judged and rejected by them all, and my extreme low self-esteem just couldn't handle it. So if I came to a social event or classroom or church situation where crowds were already in a room, I had to wait for someone to go into the room first so that I could follow them in or else I just wouldn't go in. This was obviously quite a handicap for me on a practical level but also an area of fear that I didn't want to be restricted by anymore, as I was in my twenties and wanting to do lots.

My prayer partners prayed through this with me and the Lord healed me. Then one day I faced a challenge and was about to revert to my old patterns of behaviour, but the Lord stepped in. This challenge was quite extreme but now, as I look back, I laugh at it because if I could do this, I could walk into *any* room.

My boyfriend at the time was a lovely man who was a bassist in a rock band that played the local pubs and clubs. It was the 80's and not only were there ugly stone-washed denim jeans and 'big hair' but 'rocker' and 'Hell's Angels' pubs still existed. I wanted to be a dutiful girlfriend and support him so that meant I usually became a 'roadie' (not a groupie, I'm keen to point out!) I would lug around a huge, ugly, bright orange Marshall Amplifier in the back of my minivan to all the various gigs.

However, this day I was late off my nursing shift and so couldn't arrive with the band. I suddenly realised as I got to the closed doors of this Hell's Angel pub that I was going to have to walk through the crowds. Outside men were getting drunk and quite literally falling off their parked bikes, yet inside seemed even more frightening.

I got to the closed doors of the pub. I couldn't do it! I couldn't go in! Yet I'd come all this way and my boyfriend was expecting me – this was before mobile phones. I was about to leave when I felt the Lord say very gently but firmly, 'Where are you going? Stay here. What are you doing? I've healed you. *Now walk in it.*'

*Yikes,* this was scary! Not only was I going to have to practise walking through a crowd, but this was a crowd of drunken bikers. I gritted my teeth and went in, praying as I went, 'You'd better protect me, Lord.'

I was fine. I got to my boyfriend and his friends, was welcomed and felt safe.

I then had a funny incident in the crowd, standing on my own, when his band started up. I was stood next to a small man in biker gear who looked just like Freddie Mercury except that he had a knife tucked into his belt! He pointed towards the stage and my boyfriend's band.

'This band is crap, isn't it?' He looked me full in the eye, expecting me to agree.

I looked at him and then I looked at his knife. I had a dilemma. I could either agree but be disloyal to my boyfriend or disagree and get knifed. I decided to be brave again.

'No, I think that they're good.' I braced myself for a fight or flight. True, he was short and I might be able to take him, but you never know.

He looked back at the band and then at me. 'Yes, you're quite right.'

He agreed and completely gave in! I was quite shocked but couldn't help but have a little chuckle to myself. What a wimp!

I find now that if ever I approach a closed door and I know that there's a crowd waiting, and those old fears try to push their ugly heads up, I remember that biker's pub and the man with the knife. I tell myself, if I can handle that with the Lord then I can handle most situations, and it makes me giggle. If He heals you and challenges you to walk in that healing, go for it; it will be worth it.

## Forgive us our sins as we forgive others

*Forgive as the Lord forgave you.*

*Colossians 3:13*

Probably the most important key to any healing prayer is that of beginning from a place of forgiveness. This might seem completely unreasonable; after all, if God does really care about us and wants to heal us, why on earth should we forgive our perpetrators? The answer is simply, because *He did.* Forgiving our enemies is unfortunately not just a nice idea but it is a necessity, as Jesus taught us in the Lord's prayer.[111]

---

[111] See Luke 11:4

I was still living with my father when I became a Christian at eighteen. Sometimes I would pray for protection and the abuse was avoided; sometimes I would pray and it wasn't. My father continued his abuse until he died about twenty years after my conversion. When he was no longer able to beat me, he used psychological warfare instead.

I was very blessed to receive incredible teaching and healing prayer through my first church, and forgiveness was a huge part of that.[112] Boy, did I struggle with forgiveness in those early days! How on earth could I forgive the man who had made my whole family's life an absolute, terrified misery; he who had stripped me of all self-esteem, hope, joy, comfort, faith and trust in humanity (literally)? How could I forgive the monster that reigned in that house, that tore physically and psychologically into his children's health and humanity? I prayed and prayed. *I don't understand this, Lord; how can you as a gentle, just and loving God condone this?*

Fairly quickly God answered. Forgiveness is not an emotion or even an emotional response. *It is an act of will.*

'Alison, do you *will* to forgive him because of me? You don't have to feel it, you don't even have to like it, but because it is Love's way and your way to healing, can you choose it?'

This I found much easier. God doesn't condone any human's bad behaviour; in fact, He loathes it. He doesn't condone what some men do to women or children; it breaks His heart. Yet God is a God of love, compassion and forgiveness – or none of us would be able to stand before Him, as none of us are without sin.

Does this make Him unjust, then, toward us who have been the victims of abuse? No, He has served justice through His own son, Christ. Jesus has not just taken the pain and abuse on Himself but He has also provided a way out of it, so that forgiveness is available and so that we might be set free.

Holding on to unforgiveness is, as some describe, like pouring a cup of poison for the person that caused you misery and then drinking it yourself – not helpful!

As soon as you can make that decision for forgiveness, not based on what you think is just or right, but purely because you either love Jesus

---

[112] Thank you, family in Canford Parish. Many of you have now been 'promoted to glory' but if any of you are still alive and reading this, thank you and the mighty tender God you served there. You were life-changers.

or believe God, then there is *almighty power.* You are now working in God's reign and through His kingdom. You have accessed an unbelievable key to unlock freedom and healing in your life. You might still *feel* horrible, but bad feelings can be prayed and healed away and replaced with good ones like joy, comfort, peace, faith, trust, zeal and love.[113]

## Prayer

*Dear Lord,*

*Thank you for your everlasting love for me and for the healing that you won for me upon the cross. Please would you begin this healing process in me and show me trustworthy people whom I might be able to confide in and pray with in your timing. Please would you help me to persevere in this process in your strength and to become more whole and happier than I've ever been.*

*Thank you, Lord, in Jesus' name.*

*Amen.*

---

[113] See Isaiah 61.

# CHAPTER THIRTEEN

# Jesus Believed in Emotional Healing

*There is a time for everything ... a time to heal, a time to break down and a time to build up.*

*Ecclesiastes 3:3*

Having shared with you some of my healing experiences in the last chapter, we will now look at how emotional healing works and how to access it if you're not experienced in it. We serve a just and merciful God, who wants us all to be whole and happy in our lives.

All humans have been hurt in life, therefore, all humans need healing. If you have undergone any form of abuse you will need to be healed, so why not start to access that privilege now and learn just how much God loves you?

## Jesus speaks

When Jesus begins His ministry, He stands up in the synagogue and reads these words from Isaiah 61:1-3 in the Old Testament.

*'The Spirit of the Sovereign Lord is on me, because the Lord has anointed me to preach good news to the poor. He has sent me to proclaim freedom for the prisoners and recovery of sight for the blind, to release the oppressed, to proclaim the year of the Lord's favour.'*

*Luke 4:18-19*

When He has finished reading this He states, 'Today these words are fulfilled in your presence.'[114] In other words, to paraphrase, He was

---

[114] Luke 4:21

saying to the people gathered there, 'Here I am! *This describes me!* I am the living fulfilment of all of these promises. I am not only interested in your broken heart, but I came to mend it! I have come to comfort people, to provide for them and swop hideous emotions for feelings of peace and hope. I am the only one who is able to do this! I am the one who is anointed, and I can heal you, restore you, comfort you and give you joy. I can create justice, beauty, freedom and praise, out of all that dross.'

He is the only one able to do this, because He is the only one true God. No other religion can truly offer this, because Christ is the only one who has taken all the sins and hurts of humanity upon Himself. Therefore, we have only to bring our places of hurt and pain to Him and offer them up in prayer – by faith – and He will gladly (because He loves us that much) take them and replace them with the opposite: healing, comfort, joy, restoration, redemption, peace etc. It is a type of divine exchange, our rubbish for His blessings.

## How to pray for emotional healing

*I can do everything through him who gives me strength.*

*Philippians 4:13*

This is wonderful news but how do you access this healing if you've never experienced it before? The Lord doesn't seem to work through consistent formulas for emotional healing because He respects our individuality and so will work with us each of us differently. However, there are certain biblical principles that it's good to adhere to, for healing to take place.

In the following section I explain these basic principles in ten steps. There are many wonderful books that are far more in-depth about emotional healing if you need more information (see recommended reading list). However, this is a simplified list to help you get started if you are new to this area of Christian healing.

Before we start these steps, we need to consider why and where the healing is needed. Sometimes it is obvious what has caused us emotional hurt or pain. For example, you know that you are broken-hearted by the loss of a loved one or by the end of your marriage. At other times the pain is less obvious, perhaps because we have hidden it or are in denial (often childhood hurts can be like this). Therefore, it is good to get into the habit of first asking God in which area He wants to start to heal you (this is not always the most obvious area to you).

As God answers you, memories, painful emotions and thoughts may start to surface. This might seem uncomfortable, but persevere and have some prayer support ready. Ideally, pray with others:

> *Therefore confess your sins to each other and pray for each other so that you may be healed.*

James 5:16

However, these prayer supporters need to be trustworthy and wise, and preferably experienced in this type of prayer ministry. If you don't know anyone like this, you could ask your church leaders for advice or you could go to a reliable and recommended prayer ministry. (It is important that you pray with trustworthy and honourable people as you are at your most vulnerable in this type of prayer. Ask the Lord to confirm who these people are, and if you don't feel comfortable with them, then don't continue the prayer but seek help elsewhere.)

Occasionally there may be times when you are unable to call on anyone; if so, you can still pray through this process on your own and the Lord is able to heal you just as effectively. (Though if you practise this sort of prayer, do try not to get into the habit of being a 'lone wolf' Christian. We were created for relationship, one with another, and God has built the Church as 'a body' with different gifts – including healing – so that we can love, help and look after each other.[115] This is His ideal and this type of healing prayer is far more powerful than consistently praying for this type of healing on your own.)

## 10 steps to healing

These are the recommended steps for praying for emotional healing:

### 1. CONFESS

If you know what area you need to be healed in or you have asked the Lord to show you and an area has surfaced, firstly tell the Lord and your prayer partners about what happened. Share what you felt at the time or feel about it now and how it affected you. Don't hold back any words or emotions; let it all out, however shocking or 'ungodly' it feels at the time.

---

[115] 1 Corinthians 12:27-28

## 2. FORGIVE

This is an extremely important step; in fact, *it is a necessity* and unfortunately can't be skipped.

> *'Forgive us our sins as we forgive everyone who sins against us.'*
>
> *Luke 11:4*

It may mean forgiving the person or persons who wronged you, or sometimes forgiving yourself or even the Lord. It is important to pray this out loud so that your prayer supporters can witness it before the Lord. So, for example, you might pray, 'Lord, I choose to forgive my husband for punching me in the face.'

Remember, forgiveness is a choice and a decision, not necessarily an emotion or a feeling. *In no way* does it mean that you condone the other person's bad behaviour or abuse. But it does mean that you are leaving the judgement of this person to God and that you can obtain an incredible freedom and healing through this process.

If you don't feel that you *can* forgive them, ask the Lord for His strength and to enable you to *want* to forgive them 'for my power is made perfect in weakness'[116]. This may take time and perseverance in prayer, but it will come, and in the meantime the Lord understands why you feel the way you do.

## 3. REPENT IF NECESSARY

Having granted your perpetrator forgiveness, you may need to ask God to forgive you too. Humans seldom act in a godly way in response to having been wronged. Through prayer the Lord may convict you of sinful ways in which you, however understandably, reacted to having been hurt. For example, your husband had an affair – his sin; you then keyed his car in retaliation – your sin.

If the Lord shows you that you've also sinned in a situation, admit your sin, then repent and renounce it. So, for example you might pray, 'Lord, I admit that I keyed my husband's car out of anger. I am sorry and I renounce this behaviour of seeking my own revenge on him.' To renounce it means that you are no longer choosing this behaviour as a viable option, as it is not God's way.

---

[116] 2 Corinthians 12:9

Now ask for the Lord's forgiveness and receive this forgiveness in faith. There are often no feelings to go with this forgiveness; sometimes you just have to believe and accept that this has happened. (However, occasionally I have heard of people saying that once they forgave, feelings of peace or joy came over them. Some feel physically better, others cry, others just know that it is 'sorted'.)

## 4. RENOUNCE SELF-CURSES

You may also have said to yourself, 'I'll never trust a man again!' in your understandable anger and pain. However, this is called self-cursing or making an 'inner vow', and it is something that is not helpful or right. Watch out for any 'I'll never' statements or 'I'll always', e.g. 'I'll always hate him.'

> *Do not swear – not by heaven or by earth or by anything else.*
> *Let your yes be yes and your no, no or you will be condemned.*
>
> *James 5:12*

If you do this, you are making decisions for yourself and your future that are negative, not full of faith, which is against God's ways.

> *I have set before you life and death, blessings and curses. Now choose life.*
>
> *Deuteronomy 30:19*

For example, you've stated that you'll never trust again; that means that the beautiful Christian guy whom the Lord has lined up to marry you will never be able to come near, because you've already decided your fate and you will not trust another man. Therefore, you also need to ask forgiveness for this and renounce the lie, 'I'll never trust a man again,' because until you get there and meet that man, you won't know how you feel about him or be able to recognise the blessing that God may want to give you.

## 5. SURRENDER NEGATIVE FEELINGS

In prayer, state that you are willing to literally 'give' up all of the hurting feelings (however big or small) that you have, so that Jesus can take them from you. Some people find it helpful to imagine themselves at the foot of the cross, literally 'handing over' these feelings for Him to take, by speaking each of them out and placing them at the cross or into His hands.

For example, if this had happened to you, you might pray, 'Dear Jesus, I want to give you all of the hurt I felt on the day of my nephew's wedding, when I'd made such an effort to look nice and my husband told me that I looked really ugly and fat in my dress, just as we were about to leave.'

At this point the Holy Spirit may guide you or your prayer partners with specific feelings that you need to surrender that are tied into this hurt. So, in the case of this 'wedding insult', He might show you that you also need to give up the associated feelings of rejection, insecurity about your looks, low self-esteem, humiliation, sadness, disappointment etc.

You don't need to go on a 'fishing expedition' for these feelings or try and 'work stuff up'. We all react differently even to the same situation but the Lord knows intimately how He has made you and so He will know which areas need healing.

*For you created my inmost being.*

*Psalm 139:13*

The Lord is a gentleman; He will not force you or make you give up any of your feelings you don't want to. However, if you do not open up and you leave feelings undealt-with then they will undoubtedly remain and either hinder your complete healing or will need to be dealt with at a later date.

Jesus has literally taken all of the bad feelings and sins for the whole of humanity for the whole of time. His act on the cross, although spiritual, was also based in the physical world and in time.[117] Therefore the healing you receive is real, both physically and spiritually.

*...by his wounds we are healed.*

*Isaiah 53:5*

6. BE FREED

Once you have prayed and given up these feelings, we now need to ask Jesus to set you free from them so that they no longer have power over you. There are many ways of praying this next step, but I'll just give you one example here. Once you have shown that you are willing to

---

[117] 'It is done.' (John 19:30; Revelation 21:6)

surrender the negative feelings, you then ask Jesus to set you free from them by asking Him to place His cross of crucifixion between you (heart, mind, body, soul and spirit) and the hurting emotions in order to separate and 'cut you free' from them. So, in the case of the 'wedding hurt', from the previous page, you might pray, 'Dear Jesus, thank you for having taken all of the rejection I felt at being told I looked fat and ugly. Please would you now put your cross between me and this sense of rejection and take it away from me.'

Although these prayers are in one sense metaphorical (because we have to imagine this taking place; we weren't at the Crucifixion or involved in what went on at the time) in another sense they are completely real. The act of Jesus destroying the works of evil and darkness on the cross was a definite act in earthly time and space, but it was also an act over all of eternity.

> *The reason the Son of God appeared was to destroy the devil's work.*
>
> 1 *John 3:8 (NIV)*

> *It is done. I am the Alpha and the Omega, the Beginning and the End.*
>
> *Revelation 21:6 (NIV)*

7. THE DIVINE EXCHANGE

As you have given up these negative feelings from yourself – body, mind, soul and spirit – and Jesus has set you free from them, that void needs now to be filled by God. Therefore, once these feelings have been taken, pray and ask that Jesus would cleanse you by His blood and that the power of the Holy Spirit would fill you in all the areas that have been affected by hurts and sin.

> *...and he shall give you another comforter that he may abide with you forever.*
>
> *John 16:7 (KJV)*

Next, pray and ask Jesus to fill you by the Spirit with His 'Kingdom' feelings in a swop for your 'worldly' unpleasant ones. This is the divine transaction Jesus speaks about in Isaiah 61:3: 'to bestow on them a crown of beauty instead of ashes, the oil of gladness instead of mourning, and a garment of praise instead of a spirit of despair' etc.

For example, in the case of the above 'wedding insult', the person could ask Jesus for His comfort and joy where she was hurt and sad; His acceptance and confidence where she received human rejection; and humiliation and hope and peace where she was disappointed and upset.

Again, this might have to be done purely by faith and might not have any immediate accompanying feelings. However, usually I, and people I have prayed with, report feeling different straight away. Sometimes you might have a sense of God's peace or presence, happiness or lightness, or just that the hurt has left you and you feel less sad. Sometimes you or your prayer supporters might feel that the Lord has given a 'picture' or some biblical text or a sense of how He feels about you to aid your healing. For example, He might show you how He sees you as His precious daughter, or you might sense His love for you, or He might tell you from His word that you are 'his beloved'[118]. It will be specifically for you and always encouraging.

## 8. GIVE THANKS

Having completed the 'divine exchange' prayer, do remember to give Jesus all the praise and thanksgiving that He deserves. He has freed you and taken all that sin and pain, in order that you might have life in all its fullness. He has given you a good measure, shaken down and running over;[119] be grateful to the only wise God, who is worthy.

## 9. PRAY FOR PROTECTION

After this sort of prayer, always pray for protection – protection over the healing you've received, yourself and your loved ones. The enemy comes to kill, rob and destroy all that is good.[120] He won't be happy that you have managed to step out of misery or unforgiveness into happiness, and he might use counter-attack. So 'pray on' your spiritual armour;[121] don't let him get even the slightest foothold in your healing or against your loved ones.

---

[118] from Song of Songs
[119] See Luke 6:38
[120] See John 10:10
[121] See Ephesians 6:10-18

10. REST

After deep prayer like this you might feel more peaceful or happier, or you might just feel quite washed out (as though you've had heart major surgery, which in a way you have!) It is a good idea to just be gentle with yourself for the rest of the day and not do anything too taxing or stressful – physically, mentally or spiritually.

CHAPTER FOURTEEN

# A Note to the Perpetrators

*But I tell you that anyone who is angry with his brother or
sister will be subject to judgement.*

*Matthew 5:22 (TNIV)*

I wasn't quite sure whether to include you in this book as I wanted it
to be a safe place for the readers. However, if you are a perpetrator (and
I believe that you will know if you are, despite any outward denial), I can
see only two reasons why you'd be reading this. Either you are hoping to
learn something that will help you gain more control over those you are
abusing or, hopefully, you genuinely want some help.

## Continuing to abuse

If you are planning on continuing to abuse, all I can say is, *watch out!*

I believe that there is a movement in societies across the world
(directed by the Lord God Almighty) that is starting to deal with your
issues and the consequences of your abusive actions. I believe that your
problem of abusing women is being increasingly forced out into the open.
As it is brought into the light, just societies will react and will ensure
greater justice by bringing you and your kind to account. God is quite
literally 'on your case'.

In the 'psalm' that I felt that the Lord had given me,[122] He speaks of
you. This is what He says about you:

- he loves you because you are His precious child made in His
  image;

---

[122] See chapter 9

- if, at any point, you *genuinely* desire to repent and stop this behaviour by getting help, He will forgive you;
- however, He loathes your evil behaviours and attitudes toward the women that you abuse.

You may or may not believe in the Lord God Almighty, and that of course is your choice. If you don't, then the words and experiences in this book will appear fantastical and nonsense. You will likely perceive them as no threat and will probably continue with your abuse. But just to warn you, if they are right then you will be called to account one day, whether that be on earth or in heaven, and you will have to face the consequences of your actions. Obviously if that judgement comes on earth, the consequences for you could mean prison. The choice of your destiny is yours, but really the only wise option lies in repentance and humility.

## Help for genuinely repentant believers

*If you remain in me and I in you, you will bear much fruit; apart from me you can do nothing.*

*John 15:5 (TNIV)*

There are few relationships that are as broken as those between male and female. Evidence is seen not only in divorce statistics across the world but also in female oppression regardless of faith or culture. I believe that this breaks the heart of God who intended that males and females should have an incredibly good, harmonious relationship, just as Father, Son and Spirit do within the Godhead. There is no conflict within the image of the Trinity, and humanity is made in that image.

Hopefully, if you are reading this section then you are genuinely repentant of your oppression and the conflict and hurt that you create.

Hopefully, the Lord has been convicting you that the abuse you perpetrate against your loved ones (whether that is psychological and/or physical) is a despicable sin and completely unacceptable to the God of Love.[123]

Hopefully, you are so appalled at your own behaviour that you want to get help in order to stop it, and you are willing to face anything to get it; even if that means losing your pride, wife, family, friends, work or

---

[123] See 1 John 4:16

possibly even your freedom. Hopefully, you are that serious and that resolute about it.

To honestly face your own behaviour and its consequences will probably be the most courageous and costly thing that you will ever do. But it will probably also be the most worthwhile and rewarding.

If you are *that* believer and genuinely want help, then my prayer is that the Lord will bless you mightily. Please be reassured that He is 'mighty to save'[124] everyone, including you. There are contact numbers available in the back of this book where you can get help.

## Spiritual roots

Although abuse is a complex problem, I believe that the *main roots* of this problem are spiritual (remember way back to Genesis 3, where the curse of sin is that male will want to rule over female). The roots formed in this curse are then strengthened all around us by attitudes, beliefs and behaviours in society.

Even more tragically, the desire – or sin – of males wanting to dominate females is still without doubt in some of our churches. Despite the fact that the Trinity created humanity in their own image and so created them 'male and *female*'[125], women are seen not as the image of God but as an add-on to creation, a lesser being, an afterthought, a weak 'helper', always subservient to a man. However, this idea of womankind is a lie.[126]

As Christians, through Christ we aim to live according to His kingdom values and this includes a return to life without the curses of sin and its effects. We can expect, through Christ, to break any of the curses that came through that original consequence of disobedience against God and that includes the sin of men dominating their partners or women generally.

> *Christ redeemed us from the curse of the law by becoming a curse for us.*
>
> *Galatians 3:13*

Therefore, as this sin is rooted in the spiritual, it will undoubtedly require you to pray (preferably with experienced others) to be set free

---

[124] Zephaniah 3:17
[125] Genesis 1:27 (emphasis added)
[126] If you are in doubt about this, read chapter 10.

from it. It will probably also require you to get help in several areas including being accountable, counselling, prayer support, joining specialist groups, Bible study, emotional healing and making amends.

In all of these areas you will need to persevere, and only when you have proven by time and steadfastness that the Lord has changed you, will you be able to start to ask people to trust you again. Bear in mind that this could take years or (as people have their own free will) it may never come, and that is something you will have to accept.

## What to pray

If you are genuinely repentant and wanting help, begin in prayer by repenting of all your past behaviours. Ask God for His forgiveness and then receive it in faith. Then pray and renounce this wrong belief; it is misogyny and like any bigoted belief, it is based on a lie of the enemy.

Having renounced those lies and beliefs, it would be good to pray with trusted, experienced, spiritually gifted friends or counsellors. The Lord might lead you to pray with one person initially, but if you start to pray into deeper spiritual areas, it would be wise to pray with two trusted and experienced people. Plus, it would be preferable if they believe in the equality of women.

Ask the Holy Spirit to guide you into all the areas that may need repentance or healing. He might show you that there are attitudes or characteristics that are linked to spiritual ties that might encourage you to behave in this way; for example, a link to the Freemasons, the occult or some generational sin. You may need to repent of these for yourself and your past generations, to forgive them and to renounce the beliefs and behaviours that go with these. But if you pray with experienced counsellors, they will know how this type of prayer works.

You may feel you want to apologise to those that you have hurt and to ask for their forgiveness. But I would recommend that you do this only as the Lord guides; don't be too hasty or insensitive as the wounds might still be raw for your victims.

If you are genuinely repentant and the Lord does an amazing work for you, then that will be glorious, not just for your wife and family or your future relationships, but for the world! Do you realise the power of your testimony and of how that can be used for good? This message of equality and of zero tolerance for abuse so desperately needs to be shared, and sadly that includes within the Church. Please do pray and consider how our awesome Lord might want to use the power of your story for His glory. My prayer is that if you are genuinely repentant and seeking help, that the Lord in His mercy would release, heal and bless you mightily.

## Prayer

*Lord Father God,*

*You search all things and you know my heart. As you are my witness, I am truly sorry for all of the harm that I have caused _____ [you might want to name specific people here]. I repent of these behaviours _____ [you might want to name them] and I renounce them. Please forgive me.*

*Help me to find some prayer partners whom I can pray with – to be healed by you but also to hold me to account in the future. Lord, would you please set me free to be the man you created me to be.*

*Amen.*

# Helpful Resources

This is up-to-date at the time of writing but please bear in mind that this information may change with time.

If you are at present in an abusive relationship and seeking help of any kind, especially on the Internet, please bear in mind that your abuser may check your computer or phone history to keep tabs on you. *Stay safe.* Be wise about how to hide your history (a good guide can be found on the *Refuge* website) and be mindful of where you keep paper documentation.

God be with you, an 'ever present help in times of trouble'[127].

## Books

ABOUT ABUSE

Anderson, Jocelyn; *Woman Submit!;* One Way Cafe Press (Florida, 2007). This is the personal testimony of a Christian woman who suffered abuse from her Christian husband, who was an associate pastor of their church.

Brewster, Susan; *To be an Anchor in the Storm;* Seal Press (Canada, 1997). A good guide for families or friends of abused women.

Craven, Pat; *Living with the Dominator;* Freedom Publishing (UK, 2008). This is an excellent book for recognising abusers 'types' and how to deal with them.

Engel, Beverly; *The Emotionally Abusive Relationship;* John Wiley & Sons Inc (New Jersey, 2002). This contains a programme to help couples who want to stop being emotionally abusive to each other.

Horley, Sandra; *Power and Control: Why Charming Men can make Dangerous Lovers;* Vermilion (London, 1991).

Hennessy, Don; *How He Gets into Her Head;* Cork University Press (Atrium, Ireland, 2012). This is a brilliant book written by the Director of the Cork Domestic Violence Project.

Lundy, Bancroft; *Why Does He Do That?* Penguin Books (New York, 2002). This is a useful book that covers the whole area of male abuse and helps you to recognise the signs of an abuser.

---

[127] Psalm 46:1

Penfold, Rosalind. B.; *Dragon-Slippers: This is what an Abusive Relationship Looks Like;* Penguin Group (Canada, 2005).

Roberts, Barbara; *Not Under Bondage;* Maschil Press (Australia, 2008).

Stelling, Diane; *Honour thy Father and Mother* (USA, 2003). This is a personal testimony of a woman who was abused by her parents and her path into healing.

ABOUT INNER HEALING

Bennett, Rita; *Emotionally Free;* Kingsway Publications (Eastbourne, 1982). This is out of print now but some copies can still be found online. It is a brilliant book that explains about Christian emotional healing.

Morgan, Jeannie; *Our Hands, His Healing: a Practical Guide to Prayer Ministry and Inner Healing;* Monarch Books (Oxford, 2014). An excellent book that covers all areas of healing.

Pytches, David; *Come, Holy Spirit: Learning How to Minister in Power;* Hodder & Stoughton (1987).

ABOUT THEOLOGY AND WOMEN

*http://answeringgenesis.org/human-body/from-dust-to-dust*

Anderson, Andrew (ed); *Men, Women and Authority;* Day One Publications (Bromley, Kent, 1996).

Beck, James R. and Blomberg, Craig L. (gen eds.); *Two Views on Women in Ministry;* Zondervan (Michigan, 2001).

*God's Word to Women;* http://godswordtowomen.org/ezerkenegdo.htm (2013), pages 1-2.

Guinness, Michelle; *Woman the Full Story;* Zondervan (Grand Rapids, 2003).

Kroeger Clark, Catherine and Nason-Clark, Nancy; *No Place for Abuse;* Inter-Varsity Press (USA, 2001).

Kroeger Clark, Richard and Kroeger Clark, Catherine; *I Suffer Not a Woman;* Baker Books (USA, 1992).

Perriman, Andrew; *Speaking of Women;* Apollos (England, 1988).

France, R. T.; *Women in the Church's Ministry;* Paternoster Press (Carlisle, 1995).

Strickland, Danielle; *The Liberating Truth;* Monarch (Grand Rapids, 2011).

## Abused women's organisations

Refuge: *www.refuge.org.uk*

> Refuge is the largest UK registered charity that deals with domestic violence.

AVA: *www.avaproject.org.uk*

Woman's Aid: *www.womensaid.org.uk*

Rights of Women: *www.rightsofwomen.org.uk*

> This is a voluntary organisation that deals with women's legal rights.

### CHRISTIAN ORGANISATIONS FOR ABUSED WOMEN

Restored: *www.restoredrelationships.org*

> This is a Christian alliance that aims to end violence against women worldwide but it is based in the UK and does a lot of work in the UK.

RAVE: *www.theraveproject.org*

> This group assist families of faith that have been impacted by abuse.

### ORGANISATIONS FOR EATING DISORDERS

*www.b-eat.co.uk*

*www.helenawilkinson.co.uk* (a Christian charity).

> This lady runs *Overcoming Eating Disorder* courses and has written several brilliant books on the subject.

*www.mercyministries.com*

## Abused men's organisations

Men's Advice Line: *www.menssadviceline.org.uk*

> This is a confidential helpline for men experiencing domestic violence from their partner or ex-partner.

## Organisations for perpetrators that want to stop

Respect: *www.respectphoneline.org.uk*

> This is a helpline for men who are perpetrators of domestic abuse but want to stop or for queries over someone who you may suspect to be an abuser.

Restored (as above)

# Afterword

*Therefore I am now going to allure her; I will lead her into the desert and speak tenderly to her … and will make the Valley of Achor [trouble] a door of hope.*

Hosea 2:14

### The Desert Place

I found her wandering
In the wasteland
A sad sight to see
Her hair matted and tangled
An old wound upon her knee
She was hunched
And humbled
And haunted
Her eyes a glassy stare
Her lips dry and salty
With fervent care and prayer
She'd been taken by her lover
To some barren land
And been abandoned there to wander
Without shelter or covering hand
All beauty and attraction had
Withered there and died
But He knew only there
Could her soul be magnified

I found her wandering in the wasteland
A breathless sight to see
It took some time to realise
That this Spirit-filled,
Son-kissed beauty
Was me.

# Contact the Author

To contact the author, please write to:

Alison Reid
c/o Onwards and Upwards Publishers
3 Radfords Turf
Exeter
EX5 7DX

Or send an email to:

*thebluecornflowertrust@gmail.com*

# Similar Books by the Publisher

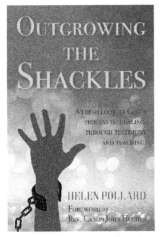

### Outgrowing the Shackles

Helen Pollard
ISBN 978-1-78815-669-1

*www.onwardsandupwards.org/outgrowing-the-shackles*

Emotional healing is often a process. God, in His infinite love and wisdom, addresses issues in our hearts in His own timing and not necessarily in the order we might choose. The freedom He brings us is not usually and instantaneous event, but a result of our growth and maturing as we allow Him to gentle touch every area of our lives.

Helen Pollard survived a traumatic childhood through Jesus' miraculous healing, alongside help from secular therapies and varied prayer ministries. In this book she uses her own story to guide us into principles that we can apply to our own lives – to outgrow the shackles. Helen's blunt realism is disarming, whilst her profound wisdom and insight into healing and forgiveness are a challenge to every believer.

### Restoring Our Hearts

Paul Collett
ISBN 978-1-907509-16-2

*www.onwardsandupwards.org/restoring-our-hearts*

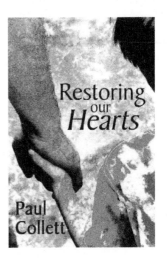

We pray to "Our Father in heaven". But many of us have had a disappointing experience of fatherhood; we have not known a good and intimate father.

In this helpful and penetrating book, Paul Collett shows some of the ways God has enabled him to overcome his own wounds and hurts. He also demonstrates that the future revival of the church will be linked to a restoration of the true meaning of fatherhood.

**Available from all good bookshops.**

Printed in Great Britain
by Amazon